PHILO'S CONTRIBUTION TO
RELIGION

PHILO'S CONTRIBUTION TO RELIGION

BY

H. A. A. KENNEDY, D.D., D.Sc.
PROFESSOR OF NEW TESTAMENT EXEGESIS,
NEW COLLEGE, EDINBURGH
AUTHOR OF
"ST. PAUL AND THE MYSTERY RELIGIONS"
"ST. PAUL'S CONCEPTIONS OF THE LAST THINGS," ETC.

WIPF & STOCK · Eugene, Oregon

Wipf and Stock Publishers
199 W 8th Ave, Suite 3
Eugene, OR 97401

Philo's Contribution to Religion
By Kennedy, H. A. A.
ISBN 13: 978-1-5326-1876-5
Publication date 3/10/2017
Previously published by Hodder and Stoughton, 1919

INSCRIBED WITH GRATITUDE
TO THE MEMORY OF
MY TWO GREAT TEACHERS
S. H. BUTCHER
AND
A. B. DAVIDSON

PREFACE

NO ancient writer of such primary importance for the environment and presuppositions of early Christianity has suffered the neglect which has fallen to the lot of Philo. This is true both of British and continental scholarship. I do not mean for a moment to underrate such comprehensive and valuable works as the late Principal Drummond's *Philo Judaeus*, 2 vols. (London : Williams & Norgate, 1888), and Dr. Emile Bréhier's *Les Idées Philosophiques et Religieuses de Philon d'Alexandrie* (Paris : A. Picard et Fils, 1908).

But Philo deserves to be made the subject of many special monographs. Possibly the sheer profusion of material has scared some competent investigators. No one, it seems to me, can attempt to penetrate the background of early Christian thought without realising the unique significance of Philo of Alexandria. And this is just as true of the practical as of the theoretical aspects of his many-sided achievement. Indeed, the chief impression made upon one by a careful reading and re-reading of his works is the extraordinary vitality of his religious interest, the depth of his religious experience. This seems to be of central value for understanding the man himself, and for estimating his bearing on Christianity.

The only attempt to examine the facts from this definite point of view, of which I am aware, is Windisch's essay, *Die Frömmigkeit Philos* (Leipzig: J. C. Hinrichs, 1909). Apart from the fact of its not being translated, the looseness and vagueness of the plan according to which the material is arranged, appeared to me likely rather to suppress than to arouse interest in one of the most remarkable figures in the history of religion. So I was emboldened to traverse the ground for myself, and to attempt to state the conclusions I had reached with as little technicality as possible. Accordingly my study is a completely independent piece of work, intended to illuminate an unusually fascinating epoch in the story of man's struggle to grasp and understand God. I have made full use of the work which has been done on Philo, but I have refrained from loading my pages either with discussions of minute details or with references to the opinions and utterances of other writers. One of my main objects has been to let Philo speak for himself.

Several of these chapters have appeared in the pages of the *Expositor*. These I have carefully revised and, where it seemed necessary, supplemented. I have cordially to thank the Editor and the Publishers of that journal for their kind permission to use them. I am also under special obligation to two friends: to Rev. J. H. Leckie, D.D., who kindly read the MS., placing at my disposal the fruits of his accurate knowledge of Philo, and to my colleague, Professor H. R. Mackintosh, D.D., D.Phil., who has helped me to correct the proofs and favoured me with valuable suggestions both as to form and contents.

H. A. A. KENNEDY.

NEW COLLEGE, EDINBURGH,
   12th September 1919.

CONTENTS

CHAPTER I
INTRODUCTION 1

CHAPTER II
PHILO'S RELATION TO THE OLD TESTAMENT . 29

CHAPTER III
FUNDAMENTAL PROBLEMS 60

CHAPTER IV
MAN'S YEARNING FOR GOD . . . 96

CHAPTER V
GOD'S APPROACH TO MAN . . . 142

CHAPTER VI
UNION WITH GOD 178

CHAPTER VII
THE MYSTICISM OF PHILO . . . 211

INDEX 239

CHAPTER I

INTRODUCTION

THE contribution which Philo of Alexandria made to spiritual religion has been largely overlooked, because attention has been focused on the philosophical significance of his thought. This was the aspect of his writings which won for him the interest of the Christian Fathers. At a time when they were eagerly seeking to bridge the gulf between the new religion and the old philosophy, which for many of them formed the chief content of their intellectual life, they found in Philo, the Jew, a thinker who had already attempted to reconcile the claims of reason and revelation. His attitude to the psychology, metaphysics and ethics of his Hellenistic environment corresponded in many respects to their own. He had not shown himself a slavish adherent of any

INTRODUCTION

single system. Probably he would have called "the most sacred Plato," as he names him, his supreme master, but he freely used what attracted him in the Pythagorean tradition, in Aristotle, in the Earlier and Middle Stoics, and in the popular *Compendia*, which must have taken a prominent place in the academic instruction of Alexandria. Philo's eclecticism naturally appealed to the Christian thinkers of the earlier centuries, for it was characteristic of the *milieu* in which they moved. They found his arguments apt for their own task of refuting Paganism.[1]

Equally acceptable in their eyes was his chosen *allegorical method*. No doubt this method had established itself in the Graeco-Roman world apart altogether from Philo. But he had employed it for a purpose parallel to that which had engrossed the Christian theologians. In his exposition of the great text-book of Judaism, the Mosaic Law, taken in its widest sense as including the patriarchal history, he had set himself as a rule to show that the details of ritual and biography were

[1] Cf. Geffcken, *Zwei Griechische Apologeten*, pp. xxv–xxxii.

INTRODUCTION

but a rich symbolism veiling the story of the soul's progress from the sense-bound life of earth to the vision of perfect reality in God. He was thus able to establish lines of communication between that ancestral religion which he reverenced so profoundly and the spiritual strivings of those Greek thinkers who had meant so much for his inner life. The great legislator of the Hebrew people had, in Philo's view, larger ends in prospect than the moral discipline of a single race. He was concerned with the elemental principles of the education of the soul for its attainment of the highest wisdom, which was nothing less than fellowship with the Existent, the fountain of all being. But that was also the goal of Hellenic philosophy. The Jewish people, therefore, had a mission to humanity. Moses was fitted to be the teacher of all aspirants after truth. The intellectual or moral difficulties of the Old Testament vanished when the proper standard of interpretation was applied to them. No material was left for the contemptuous criticism of pagan philosophers.

INTRODUCTION

The Fathers of the Church availed themselves of Philo's method for their own purposes. The Old Testament had already proved one of the most powerful instruments in the Christian mission. It had to a large extent provided the new faith with a religious vocabulary. It formed the background of those conceptions which, in writings like the Epistles of St. Paul and the Fourth Gospel, created the basis of a Christian theology. The religious experience it recorded was truly felt to be consummated in Jesus Christ. But the inevitable controversy with Judaism demanded something more. For the champions of the older religion also found their weapons in the sacred book. From the beginning, the early Church had searched the Old Testament for anticipations of its fundamental truths. By the use of Philo's principles of interpretation, it became possible to demonstrate that from Genesis to Malachi, through history and ceremonial, the Scriptures had exclusive reference to "the good things to come."

For such reasons as these the study of

INTRODUCTION

Philo has suffered from a lack of proportion. He has been treated either as the most important representative of a curious blend of Jewish monotheism with later Greek eclecticism, that is, as an interesting link in the long chain of speculation on the philosophy of religion in its widest sense, or as the chief exponent of a fantastic method of interpreting documents which can scarcely excite even the archaeological interest of the modern world. Abnormal attention has been directed to his fluid and confused conceptions of the Divine Logos and the Divine Powers. His ethical positions have been mainly estimated in the light of their relation to contemporary Stoicism. Serious attempts have been made to force his often vague and contradictory speculations into the rigid framework of a system of metaphysics. Ridicule has been poured upon his quaint handling of patriarchal names and grammatical details of the Greek Old Testament. But these are not the things that count in Philo. He is only to a slight extent important as the architect of a structure of doctrine,

INTRODUCTION

philosophical or religious, if he ever aimed at such an achievement. His *speculative* effort to bring God into touch with the world of men through λόγος or δυνάμεις or ἄγγελοι is no more successful than that of his revered master, Plato, so vastly his superior in constructive intellecual power, to relate his Ideas to the realm of actual experience. Many of his dicta on the Divine essence, the constitution of the cosmos, the soul of man and its origin, the processes of life, and the nature of society have become hopelessly antiquated.

Nevertheless Philo stands out as one of the landmarks in the history of religion. His career lies on the boundaries between the old world and the new. Born not later, in all probability, than 20 B.C., and dying some time after 41 A.D., possibly not until the fifth decade of our era, he was a contemporary both of Jesus and of Paul. These facts alone mark his significance for students of early Christianity. On the *nature* of that significance we must briefly dwell.

Needless to say, there is no trace of acquaintance on his part with Jesus or His

INTRODUCTION

foremost apostle. We cannot tell whether he ever came into contact with the Christian faith. The tradition of his meeting Peter at Rome (Eus. *H.E.* II. 17. 1 ; Photius, *Biblioth.* Cod. 105 ; Suidas, *s.v.* Φίλων) seems to be purely legendary, based apparently on the notion that the Therapeutae, whom he describes in the *De Vita Contemplativa*, were followers of Mark, the disciple of Peter. But for the life and thought of that Graeco-Roman world to which Christianity made its appeal, he is in many respects a witness of the first importance. The sidelights thrown by his writings upon his Hellenistic environment have never been adequately estimated. His references to mystery-religion, to pagan festivals, to the widespread influence of astrology, to the dominant ideas of fate, to the current practices of "mantic"; his comments on Greek education, on the function of rhetoric and dialectic, on current political thought and existing scientific beliefs, are invaluable for the reconstruction of an all-important period. But far above this more or less incidental interest is his position as a

INTRODUCTION

Hellenistic Jewish thinker, whose life was spent at Alexandria, probably at that time the most remarkable centre of religious ferment in the Eastern world. It has been customary for scholars (*e.g.* Bousset) to treat Philo as a completely isolated phenomenon. This seems to us an abuse of the argument from silence. Unquestionably his individuality is unique. But, as Bousset himself admits, Philo gives many hints that he stands in a line of religious philosophers of Jewish birth, who combined devotion to the sacred tradition of their race with the wider outlook opened to them by contemporary Hellenistic speculation.[1] We naturally think in this connection of the author or (as it is probably a composite work) authors of the *Wisdom of Solomon*, which most scholars assign to the *milieu* of Alexandria. But this document is a genuine product of the developed Wisdom-literature of the Jews. It is philosophical

---

[1] *Jüdisch-Christliche Schul-betrieb*, pp. 153, 154. It seems to us that Bousset's source-criticism of *Leg. Alleg.* ii. and iii. (*op. cit.* p. 82 f.), and of *De Congress. Erud. Gr.* (p. 109 f.), governed by this standpoint, is far too subjective to be relied on.

INTRODUCTION

only to a very limited degree. No doubt its conception of Wisdom often coincides with the Reason of the Stoics as the all-pervading πνεῦμα of the universe. And the famous description in chap. vii. 22 ff. would at many points cohere with Philo's doctrine of the Logos. But the thought of the book has not been steeped in Greek metaphysics, as Philo's has been, and what is perhaps the most noteworthy element in it, the remarkable stress laid on the hope of immortality, belongs to a province not specially cultivated by the later thinker. Hence it would be illegitimate to group these authors, at any rate, in a single school. A large amount of the material embodied in Philo's voluminous writings is quite obviously inherited tradition.[1] It appears often in the same form, occasionally with slight variations, in the compilers who abounded after the creative epoch of Greek philosophy had spent its force.[2] As incorporated in *Compendia*, it was probably familiar to many of his fellow-

---

[1] See Bousset, *op. cit.*, *e.g.* pp. 14 ff., 23, 153.
[2] See, *e.g.*, Schmekel, *Die Mittlere Stoa*, pp. 409–428.

INTRODUCTION

countrymen who, like himself, had passed through a curriculum of Greek education. But in Philo's case the search for truth was a consuming passion. His facile pen was not daunted by any nice feeling for style. His cumbrous and careless paragraphs are indeed often left threadbare with repetition. But when his spirit kindles, his language takes fire, and the tedium of fine-spun speculation is overshadowed by the glimpse of a soul rapt up to the vision of God.

It may help us to a truer estimate of Philo's thought and experience if we take a brief glance at the *personality* of the man. That is made comparatively easy by his self-revealing tendency. There is a frankness and artlessness about his attitude towards men and things which give careful readers of his books a sense of real acquaintance with their author. This intimacy does not mean the mere satisfying of curiosity as to his tastes and pursuits, his prejudices or his enthusiasms. It creates a feeling of affectionate friendliness. Here is a man of lofty ideals, of unwearying zeal in the quest for

INTRODUCTION

goodness and truth : one who can turn his back on the lower aspects of the life of sense and keep himself "unspotted from the world." Yet he assumes no airs. He takes his readers into his confidence. If they are willing to overlook a diffuseness which often irritates, both in thought and style, and a frequent cumbrousness of expression which lays a burden on the attention, they may dwell in a quiet, homely atmosphere with a mind that is wholesome and refined, a spirit which sends forth ennobling influences, and leaves on sympathetic listeners the impression that they have been in pure and stimulating company.

In one of those notable glimpses which Philo gives us of his own experience, he describes with pathos his unmixed delight in the contemplation of the world and God, a condition in which he felt himself lifted high above the worries of mortal life. But an evil fate, jealous of his felicity, was lying in wait to plunge him into the sea of turbulent political anxieties. This hard lot was inevitable. All he can now do is to thank

INTRODUCTION

God that he is not completely engulfed in the billows; that he can still open the eyes of his soul to the light of wisdom (*De Spec. Leg.* iii. 1 ff.). The fervour of his utterance is sufficient evidence of its sincerity. Yet no responsive reader can think of Philo as a recluse. A life of self-control and self-dedication to the claims of religious contemplation is certainly his ideal. But no man was ever more alive to the varied play and colour of the world about him, and the society of which he formed a part. His temperament is keenly sensitive. He has followed with absorbing interest the coming forth of bud and leaf in spring (*Quod Deus sit immut.* 38 f.). He is fascinated by the beauty of light (e.g. *De Abr.* 156 ff.; *De Ebriet.* 44), in which he finds a continual source of illustrations of spiritual processes. He has carefully watched the vicissitudes of ships both in calm and stormy seas, and can make effective use of his observations to delineate the fortunes of the soul (e.g. *De Cherub.* 37 f.; *De Migr. Abr.* 6; *De Post. Cain.* 22). Music appeals to him, and he has some knowledge

INTRODUCTION

of harmony (e.g. *De Post. Cain.* 105 f.; *De Cherub.* 110). He has an intimate acquaintance with the athletic festivals of the Graeco-Roman world, and has studied the efforts and aims of the competitors (e.g. *De Agric.* 111 ff.; *De Cherub.* 81 ff.). He has frequented the theatre, and carried away clear, shrewd impressions (*De Ebriet.* 49 ff.). He is a man of general cultivation, who has felt the charm of the great art of Pheidias (*De Ebriet.* 89), and can make apt quotations from Homer and Euripides when occasion calls. He shows a thorough knowledge of the ordinary curriculum of Greek education, and is able to discuss its details with insight (e.g. *De Ebriet.* 49 ff.; *De Congress. Erud.* 15 ff.; *De Somn.* i. 205). He reveals a quite definite interest in medicine (e.g. *Quod Deus sit immut.* 65 f.; *De Sacrif. Ab.* 123), and Bréhier believes that he had taken a medical course (*Les Idées phil. et relig. de Philon*, p. 286 and *n.* 6).

His outlook upon ordinary life is sane and penetrating. He has reflected much on politics, and his remarks on the statesman

INTRODUCTION

(e.g. *De Joseph.* 32 ff., 54 ff.) are the well-weighed product of ripe observation. He gives vivid, caustic estimates of the familiar figure of the sophist (e.g. *De Congr. Erud.* 67 f.; *Quod det. pot.* 72 f.; *De Agric.* 136). He is aware of the vulgar extravagances of the wealthy (*De Fuga*, 28 ff.), and of the follies of reckless luxury (*De Somn.* ii. 48 ff.). And the pointed appeal which he makes to money-lenders as a class lifts the veil from a corner of the social life of the time. But he is an observer also of the more elusive aspects of human intercourse, a fact indicated, for example, by the illuminating things he has to say on the reflection of a man's moods in his eyes (*De Abr.* 151). It would take too long even barely to outline his wide knowledge of the natural sciences of his day, as exemplified, to mention only one department, by his frequent references to the laws which govern the movements of the heavenly bodies. But perhaps enough has been said to emphasise the mental alertness, the moral balance, and the real lovableness of this remarkable Jewish Hellenist who

INTRODUCTION

stood on the threshold of a new and wonderful epoch.

Yet before we leave this phase of our subject, we feel compelled to illustrate by one or two passages the *poetic* aspect of Philo's temperament, so fundamental for his thinking, and so strangely overlooked.

In the first which we shall quote, he is making an impassioned protest against the evil fortune which suddenly plunged him, in the midst of his meditation on the highest things, into the whirlpool of political life. He has not been completely swept away. "There are moments when I raise my head, and with spiritual eyesight bedimmed (for the keen glance of the soul has been clouded by the haze of alien interests), gaze around, with ardent yearning for a pure and untroubled life. And then, if there be granted me, without looking for it, a brief calm and respite from political turmoil, I soar aloft in winged flight, well-nigh treading the air, breathing the breath of Knowledge, which ever urges me to flee to her converse as from harsh taskmasters, not men alone, but the torrent

INTRODUCTION

of affairs that surges in upon me from every side. Nevertheless it is meet to give thanks to God that, despite my struggle with the flood, I am not engulfed in its depths, but may open the eyes of my soul which, in despair of all bright hope, I deemed to be fast closed, and am illumined by the radiance of wisdom, not delivered over for ever to the sway of darkness" (*De Spec. Leg.* iii. 4–6). For Philo the heights of wisdom and knowledge are only to be attained in communion with God. And it is when the sense of God and His goodness to the soul breaks upon him that his utterance is exalted to a poetic strain, the expression of a high passion. "If a yearning come upon thee, O soul, to possess the good, which is Divine, forsake not only thy 'country,' the body, and thy 'kindred,' the sense-life, and thy 'father's house,' the reason, but flee from thyself, and depart out of thyself, in a Divine madness of prophetic inspiration, as those possessed with Corybantic frenzy. For that high lot becomes thine when the understanding is rapt in ecstasy, feverishly agitated with a heavenly passion,

INTRODUCTION

beside itself, driven by the power of him who is True Being, drawn upwards towards him, while truth leads the way" (*Quis Rer. Div. H.* 69, 70). Notably does his wonder in presence of the Divine grace break out in hymns of praise. "Bounteous, O Lover of giving, are thy kindnesses, without limit or boundary or end, as fountains which pour forth streams too plentiful to be carried away" (*op. cit.* 31). And again: "O mighty Lord, how shall we praise thee, with what lips, with what tongue, with what speech, with what governing power of the spirit? Can the stars, blended in single chorus, chant thee a worthy anthem? Can the whole heaven, melted into sound, declare even a portion of thine excellences?" (*De Vita Mos.* ii. (iii.) 239). At times the rapture of his spirit imparts a fresh glow to Nature. "The soul anticipates its expectation of God," he says, "with an early joy. We may liken it to that which happens with plants. For these, when they are to bear fruit, first bud and blossom and put forth shoots. Look at the vine, how wondrously Nature has decked it out with slender twigs and tendrils, with

INTRODUCTION

suckers and leaves, which all but utter in living accent the joy of the tree over the fruit that is to come. The day, too, laughs at early dawn, as it waits for the sun-rising. For there is a first heralding of the sun's beams, and a dimmer radiance proclaims the fuller blaze" (*De Mut. Nom.* 161 f.). This poetic feeling gives us a truer clue to the soul of the man than most of his favourite speculations. It reveals his profound kinship, on the one hand with the Psalmists of his race, on the other with his Greek master, Plato, in the deepest reaches of the inner life. It belongs indissolubly to that mystic "enthusiasm" which was so dominant a force in all his aspirations, and which pervades his religion at its highest. His search for God glows with a radiant ardour, the reflection of a spirit that thrills to the finest issues.

Here, then, is a devout Jewish thinker, the groundwork of whose spiritual life is the religion of the Old Testament. Never for a moment does he swerve from his allegiance to that sacred tradition. Never does he grow weary of extolling the Divine legislation of

INTRODUCTION

which Moses has been the mouthpiece. But he is a genuine product of the Diaspora. We know that Egypt was not only one of the earliest countries to admit Jews to its hospitality, but that there special privileges were accorded to them. That must have counted for much in their attitude to the Hellenistic environment created by Alexander's conquests, and the movements that followed them. It was probably customary at Alexandria, with its famous schools of learning, for Jews of intellectual bent to avail themselves of " the general education " (ἡ ἐγκύκλιος παιδεία) current in Greek society. In any case Philo valued both the introductory course, and the profounder study of philosophy which came later. We have few data from which to reconstruct his actual curriculum. Part of it he probably received within his own community. But it is difficult to avoid the conclusion that he had come into personal touch with the philosophical schools of the great "University" of the city in which his life was spent.

What is of paramount interest for us is to

INTRODUCTION

observe carefully the effect of the impact of Greek ideas upon this sensitive religious mind. Did they produce serious modifications in his inherited conceptions of God, of God's relations to men, of human nature, of the purpose of life? How far could a loyal Jew be affected by contemporary notions of the fundamental elements of experience, such as matter and spirit, reason, moral obligation and the like? To what extent were the spiritual values of the Old Testament replaced by others? Does the process reveal a preparation for or approximation to the Christian view of God and the world? Such questions form one aspect of our inquiry. And they must come up again and again in our examination of the main subject before us, the contribution of Philo to religion. But throughout the discussion we wish deliberately to reckon with the phenomena of the New Testament. There we are confronted by what is, in some important respects, a parallel situation. The Letters of Paul, the Epistle to the Hebrews, and the Fourth Gospel are also the products of devout Jewish minds. They

INTRODUCTION

all spring from an Old Testament soil. But they all presuppose a Hellenistic environment. Their authors have been more or less in touch with the currents of contemporary thought, and they have to meet the needs of Jews like themselves who have burst the bonds of a rigid Judaism, as well as of Gentiles, whom pagan religion, even in its highest forms, has failed to satisfy. How far has there been a reaction to Greek thought on their part? Has that thought penetrated their central categories? Has it reshaped to any degree their working conceptions of God and His contact with human life? Or, has their experience of Jesus Christ so completely overshadowed every other force in their religion as practically to neutralise the power of environment? We know that conflicting answers are being given to these questions at the present time. Perhaps a comparison at salient points with the positions of Philo will help to illuminate the situation. At least, it may clear away some misconceptions and suggest a more accurate perspective.

What has been said serves roughly to

INTRODUCTION

determine the nature of our proposed investigation. The works of Philo form a sort of encyclopaedia of ancient philosophical ideas, of results, often naïve enough, attained by the science of his day, of traditional lore, Hellenistic and Jewish, of spiritual experiences of his own which have the perennial fascination of real life. Much of this material we deliberately ignore. We have no intention of examining the bearings of his philosophical standpoint as a whole. Nor does it lie within our scope to discuss systematically even such central conceptions as that of God or the Universe or the Logos or νοῦς or the Moral Ideal. Our chief aim is to sketch, however fragmentarily, *making constant use of his own words*, the contribution which this loyal, earnest and highly cultivated Jewish thinker made to religion at the very time when Jesus appeared with His Gospel of the Fatherhood of God and a Divine Kingdom not of this world, won through suffering and death: when the followers of Jesus Christ carried through the Diaspora the message of a new relation to God, made possible through

INTRODUCTION

Christ crucified and risen. As has been indicated, we desire to relate our discussion at one point and another to the New Testament material. That does not mean the endeavour to search out groups of parallel ideas or formulas in Philo and the great New Testament writers.[1] Such a task has frequently been attempted in one form or other, and it is doubtful whether it has led to important results. So much depends on the contexts of the passages singled out and the background against which they stand. And these are features of the situation which have usually been ignored. It would seem more profitable to examine carefully certain integral elements in the fabric of Philo's religion for their own sake, endeavouring with caution to estimate the forces which have shaped them, and then to try to discover in what relation they stand to corresponding New Testament conceptions. If the material be properly selected, each ought to shed light on its parallel. And there is the advantage

[1] Cf. Jowett's essay on "St. Paul and Philo," in his *Commentary on Thessalonians, Galatians and Romans*, vol. i.

INTRODUCTION

in both cases that the Old Testament contributes a common background.

The masterly edition of Philo's works by Cohn, Wendland and Reiter (of which six volumes have appeared, Berlin, 1896–1915), one of the finest achievements of modern scholarship, provides a thoroughly trustworthy basis of investigation, with the addition of the *Quaestiones in Genesim* and *in Exodum*, translated from the Armenian into Latin by J. B. Aucher.[1] The only treatise in Cohn's edition of whose genuineness we are not convinced is the *De Aeternitate Mundi*, which has far more the appearance of a somewhat superficial compilation than any of the other documents. A vigorous attack on its authenticity may be found in the *Quellenstudien zu Philo von Alexandria* of so highly equipped a scholar as H. von Arnim (*Philologische Untersuchungen*, ed. by Kiessling u. Wilamowitz, Berlin, 1888), pp. 1–52. But this is not the place either to embark on source-criticism or to investigate the development of

---

[1] In the *Quaestiones* we have used the Leipzig ed. of Philo (1829–30), vols. vi.–vii.

INTRODUCTION

Philo's ideas by attempting a chronological arrangement of his works. The most interesting essay in that direction is Cohn's article, "Einleitung u. Chronologie der Schriften Philo's," in *Philologus*, Supplem. Bd. vii., 1899.

It seems advisable to begin by emphasising the more characteristic features of Philo's relation to the Old Testament. We do not propose to spend time on the details of his allegorical method, except in so far as these may illuminate various corresponding features in the Pauline Epistles and the Fourth Gospel But his general attitude to the Law and the Prophets is important for the entire discussion, and his doctrine of verbal inspiration not only raises some curious problem for his own writings, but has a bearing on certain remarkable phenomena in the New Testament.

Every large-minded religious thinker is bound to relate his positions to various philosophical assumptions more or less consciously recognised. This is especially true of one like Philo, for whom philosophy had opened up a new universe. Contradictions may often be traced among such assumptions, contradic-

INTRODUCTION

tions which have scarcely been realised by the philosophical theologian himself. In ancient thought, moreover, which preserved survivals of primitive religion and primitive science, these discrepancies were bound to remain for long undetected. The risk was intensified in the case of a devout Jew, whose enthusiasm for the efforts of Greek speculation concealed from him the fact that he was constantly attempting to fuse together incompatible magnitudes. But granting all this, it ought to repay us to examine his attitude to such fundamental problems as the relation of God and the world and the constitution of human nature, not merely for the purpose of discovering how far Hellenistic thought influenced his ultimate postulates, but also for the purpose of ascertaining what points of contact, if any, may emerge between him and his Hellenistic-Jewish contemporary, Paul of Tarsus, who had also seriously reflected on these very questions.

Our supreme interest, however, attaches to Philo's religion. That presupposes man's yearning for God and God's approach to

INTRODUCTION

man. Here it is above all else important to investigate, on the one hand, his conception of the Divine grace in the wide range of its activities, and on the other, the obstacles which thwart the human soul and deaden its sensitiveness to higher influences, in a word, the many-sided phenomena of the inner life which may be grouped under such categories as sin, conscience, repentance and faith. This, further, is the sphere to which would belong a consideration, however fragmentary, of Philo's doctrine of the Logos. That doctrine, as we have hinted, is riddled with contradictions. But the idea of mediators between God and the world is so central for Philo (as it was for his pagan and Jewish contemporaries) in one form or other, that we must briefly touch upon a few of its salient aspects, keeping in view at the same time the New Testament parallels, and especially the all-important Biblical conception of the Spirit of God.

We shall then be in a position to deal with the crowning-point of Philo's religious aspiration, union with God. A wide vista is here

INTRODUCTION

opened up. The content embraced in it is far from being co-ordinated. It consists of sudden flashes of insight and exaltation. In these Philo reveals the depths of his religious consciousness as nowhere else. But intuitions defy analysis. The most sacred type of feeling cannot be dissected. We must be content with examining some presuppositions of this high attainment. The pathway will thus be prepared for approaching the author's crowning doctrine of the Vision of God. Our investigation will be rounded off by a brief discussion of Philo's mysticism and the inspiration and ecstasy which are its conditions.

CHAPTER II

PHILO'S RELATION TO THE OLD TESTAMENT

NO more instructive summary could be given of Philo's general attitude towards the Old Testament than that which appears in his own remarkable statement of Moses' various functions as leader of Israel. "We have already argued," he says, "that the perfectly-equipped leader must have four functions assigned to him, the kingly, the legislative, the priestly, and the prophetic, that as legislator he may enjoin what ought to be done and forbid what ought not, that as priest he may deal not only with human but also with Divine matters, that as prophet he may reveal what cannot be grasped by reason. As I have discussed the first three of these, and proved that Moses excelled as king and legislator and high priest, I come finally to show that he was also the most notable of prophets. I thus recognise that all that stands written in the sacred books are Divine oracles, declared through him, and I will go on to details, after making this observation : of these sacred utterances some were spoken by God in person, using His marvellous prophet as interpreter, some were revealed as the result of question and answer, and some were announced by Moses in person, in a state of inspiration and possession " (*De Vita Mos.* ii. (iii.) 187 f.).

Various features here are significant. Moses is the supreme figure in the history of the chosen people. He has been used as the special medium of the Divine revelation to Israel. What he has written in the sacred books possesses Divine authority. The statement makes it clear that for Philo the Pentateuch is the kernel of the Old Testament, and that it is in the most literal sense inspired. We shall not discuss at this stage Philo's conception of inspiration. But in order to realise its scope, it must be observed that he assigns the same infallibility to the Septuagint translation as that which belongs

THE OLD TESTAMENT

to the original. He accepts the Jewish legend as to the miraculous agreement of all the translators, working separately, in their renderings, and observes that these men must be called "not translators but hierophants and prophets, inasmuch as it was granted to them by unalloyed reasonings to coincide with the wholly pure spirit of Moses" (*op. cit.* ii. 40). We may note in passing that it is the translation of the laws which is especially before his mind (*op. cit.* ii. 36).

Philo's chief aim in all his works, it need scarcely be said, is to demonstrate the universal validity of Jewish religion as enshrined in the Old Testament, and, *par excellence*, in the Pentateuch. Probably he devotes himself to this task for his own sake, for that of his co-religionists, and to win the attention of his Hellenistic contemporaries. In his own case the extraordinary fascination of Greek philosophy for his mind perhaps compelled him to adjust the powerful claims of reason to the authority of what he regarded as a Divine revelation. A similar adjustment would be needful for many of his fellow-countrymen who

PHILO'S RELATION TO

had passed through experiences like his own. And it was natural for him to appeal along these lines to fair-minded pagans, in whose rich heritage of wisdom he shared, but who, he felt, had lessons of incalculable value to learn from the Divinely-taught philosophy of Moses.

But the work was beset by difficulties. Although he never challenged the assumption of verbal inspiration, he could no longer approach the sacred text with the artlessness of unquestioning submission. Thus when he reads in Gen. ii. 8 that "God planted a garden in Eden," he remarks: "To suppose that vines and olive-trees or apple-trees . . . were planted by God is utter and incurable stupidity. . . . We must therefore have recourse to allegory, the favourite method of men of vision" (*De Plant.* 32 ff.). There can be little question that Philo stood in a long succession of allegorical interpreters of the Old Testament. The practice had been reduced to a kind of science.[1] This he

---

[1] At the same time, Siegfried's list of allegorical canons (*Philo von Alexandria als Ausleger d. A.T.*, pp. 168–197) assumes a rigidity of practice for which we have no adequate evidence.

THE OLD TESTAMENT

assumes. "Do not be surprised," he says, quite incidentally, "if, according to the rules (κανόνας) of allegory, the sun is identified [in Gen. xxviii. 11] with the Father and Governor of the universe" (*De Somn*. i. 73). Numerous references of the same character occur in his writings. A large variety of competing interpretations is current and familiar to Philo. In discussing, *e.g.*, the phrase used of Abraham (Gen. xv. 15), "Thou shalt depart to *thy fathers*," he mentions three differing explanations of "thy fathers": "Some say, the sun and moon and the other stars. . . . Some think of the archetypal Ideas. . . . Some have conjectured that the four elements are meant of which the universe is composed" (*Quis Rer. Div. H.* 280 ff.). Occasionally he speaks of his predecessors in this art. as φυσικοὶ ἄνδρες (e.g. *De Abr*. 99; *De Vita Mos*. ii. (iii.) 103), sometimes, as in the quotation above, as ὁρατικοί. Apparently, therefore, he was in possession of an elaborately articulated system of allegorical exegesis, although he does not hesitate again and again to suggest

PHILO'S RELATION TO

interpretations of his own (see esp. the remarkable passage, *De Cherub.* 27 ff.). Hence we need not be surprised to come upon the statement: "Practically everything, or at least most things, in our legislation must be taken allegorically" (*De Joseph.* 28). Philo acts consistently upon this principle, and his theory of allegory is worthy of a brief notice. It is essentially esoteric in character, and this presupposes a certain initiation, if its application is to be grasped. In introducing a complicated allegorical explanation of the sacrifice of Isaac which Abraham was ready to carry out, he says: "The story as a matter of fact does not rest upon the literal and obvious version, so that to the average reader its nature seems rather obscure, but those who have an understanding for the invisible things of the mind rather than for the perceptions of the senses and who possess the power of vision, recognise it" (*De Abr.* 200). That is the reason why once and again he appeals to his readers in the language of the Mysteries, e.g. *Leg. All.* iii. 209: "Open

THE OLD TESTAMENT

your ears, O ye initiates, and receive the mystic ritual."

Plainly, his method enables Philo to remove innumerable stumbling-blocks from the sacred narratives: *e.g.* to take literally the statement of Gen. xi. 5, that "the Lord came down to view the city and the tower," is "monstrous impiety." For "who is not aware that one who comes down must leave one part of space and occupy another. But the whole universe is filled by God" (*De Confus. Ling.* 135 f.). The startling character of the phrase can only be explained, as in other cases, by the legislator's need of using human speech about a God who is not anthropomorphic, to assist men's spiritual education (*op. cit.* 134 f.). The real explanation lies beneath the surface. An obstacle of a less serious type is found in Jacob's command to Joseph to visit his brethren in Sychem (Gen. xxxvii. 13). "How could any one in his senses accept such a situation? Is it likely that a man with such kingly resources as Jacob should have such a scarcity of slaves or servants that he must send his son abroad" on errands of this kind? (*Quod det. pot. insid.* 13). Here also trained insight is necessary. Yet Philo's practice is by no means uniform. Thus to a very large extent he treats the story of Abraham's obedience in the sacrifice of Isaac as a historical narrative, and gives an elaborate exposition of it on that basis (*De Abr.* 167-199). The early life of Joseph is similarly handled as actual history (*De Joseph.* 1-27), although its allegorical exegesis follows. Indeed, in *De Migr. Abr.* 89, he goes the length of saying: " There have been some who, regarding the literal laws as symbols of ideal realities, were excessively scrupulous in some points, while in others they were lazily negligent. For my own part I must blame such people for their laxity. For both elements demand attention, the most diligent search for hidden meanings, and the preservation of those on the surface which cannot be challenged." The literal sense he compares in this passage to the body, the symbolic to the soul (*op. cit.* 93). The comparison explains the well-known statement of Clement of Alexandria regard-

THE OLD TESTAMENT

ing the Fourth Gospel (Eus. *H.E.* vi. 14):
"John, last of all, having perceived that the
bodily things had been set forth in the
Gospels, being urged by his friends, inspired
by the Spirit, produced a spiritual Gospel";
and indirectly supplies the clue to much that
is enigmatic and baffling throughout that
book. In agreement with this frequently
close adherence to the literal narrative is the
emphasis Philo lays on minute verbal points.
He finds, *e.g.*, in Ex. xxi. 12 the law: "If
a man strike another and he die, he must
certainly be put to death" (θανάτῳ θανατούσθαι).
"Being clearly aware," he proceeds, "that he
[Moses] never uses a superfluous word. . . .
I was puzzled by his saying of the voluntary slayer not only θανατοῦσθαι but θανάτῳ
θανατοῦσθαι. . . . But when I consulted that
wise woman whose name is Enquiry, I was
relieved from my search : for she taught me
that some living people are really dead, while
some who have died are truly alive" (*De Fuga*,
54 f.). Similarly, in the opening paragraphs
of *De Agricult.* he urges the minute accuracy
of Moses in his use of terms, and presses the

PHILO'S RELATION TO

distinction between γεωργία, husbandry, and γῆς ἐργασία, the working of land.[1]

Yet there are other features of his usage which seem directly to conflict with this microscopic attention to detail. An extraordinary example is his manner of quoting from the LXX. We have seen that he held the translation to be verbally inspired. Nevertheless he handles the infallible text with the utmost freedom. Often, in citing a passage, he gives part of it in his own words: *e.g.* in Gen. xv. 6, for the clause, "it was counted to him for righteousness," he substitutes, "he was considered righteous." More daringly still, he sometimes without warning replaces the very words he is supposed to be interpreting by his own allegorical explanation: *e.g.* in Num. v. 2: "Let them send away *out of the camp* every leper," he substitutes for τῆς παρεμβολῆς

[1] In the light of these and many parallel phenomena, it seems by no means legitimate to draw the sharp distinction which Bousset does between the Palestinian Rabbinic exegesis and that of Alexandria, and to say that the one is of the letter, while the other is of the spirit (*Die Religion d. Judentums*[2], p. 185). The Rabbinic scrupulousness about verbal minutiae has unquestionably influenced Philo.

THE OLD TESTAMENT

the phrase, τῆς ἁγίου ψυχῆς, "the consecrated soul." Repeatedly he exchanges a less for a more familiar word, and often omits unimportant expressions altogether.[1] Equally remarkable, in view of his standpoint, are such statements as that which he makes regarding the creation of Eve. In expounding Gen. ii. 21, "And he took a rib," etc., he remarks: "The literal narrative in this case is mythical, for, could anybody accept the story that woman was made out of the rib of a man?" (*Leg. Alleg.* ii. 19). So also, in speaking of Moses' fiery serpents, which call up the story of the serpent's deception of Eve, he describes them as prodigies, and adds: "But in explanations based on the hidden sense, the mythical element disappears, and the truth is made evident" (*De Agricult.* 96 f.). Here is a definite recognition of myth in the patriarchal narratives.

How are we to relate these features of his attitude towards the text to his doctrine of verbal inspiration? As a matter of fact, they

[1] These instances are taken from Bishop Ryle's most useful discussion, *Philo and Holy Scripture*, pp. xxxv–xxxviii.

are wholly irreconcilable. Without realising what had happened, Philo, by his adoption of the allegorical method, had emptied his basal doctrine of all genuine value. By continuing to emphasise verbal details, he presented, indeed, the appearance of loyalty to his fundamental assumption, and probably he concealed from himself the implications of his normative system. Hence, whatever language he might still use, in reality he accepted as much of the literal text as suited his scheme of thought, and had no hesitation in explaining away what proved incompatible with that.

A comparison with St. Paul's standpoint at once presses itself on our attention. For the same kind of difficulty confronts him in a parallel situation. Very rarely, indeed, does the Apostle have recourse to the allegorical method, which was evidently familiar to him. The most notable instance is, of course, the allegory of the two Covenants, under the names of Sarah and her handmaid, Hagar (Gal. iv. 21–31), the mistress symbolising the heavenly Jerusalem, the free

THE OLD TESTAMENT

community of Christians, the slave representing the earthly centre of Judaism, which remains in the bondage of legalism. Philo more than once allegorises the same story, but, as we should expect, on totally different lines (*De Congress. Erud. Grat.*, esp. 11–24). Thus for him, Sarah stands for complete virtue, with whom Abraham, the "learner," cannot at first be fruitfully united. He must first wed Hagar, *i.e.* preliminary instruction. Later on, his marriage with virtue will bring forth fruit. A precisely similar use of the story is made by him in *Quaestt. in Gen.* iii. pp. 190–191. So far as historical sense is concerned, there is little difference between the two writers. To say, as Lightfoot does (*Galatians*, p. 199), that "Philo is, as usual, wholly unhistorical," while with "St. Paul, on the other hand, Hagar's career is an allegory, because it is a history," is to ignore the fact that Hagar's "history" has no connection of any kind with existing Judaism, and Paul's use of it is as arbitrary on its own lines as Philo's. A remarkably close correspondence of standpoint is exhibited by a comparison of Paul's position in 1 Cor. ix. 9–10 with that of Philo in *De Sacrific.* 260. The Apostle, in defending the right of missionaries to be supported by the communities in which they labour, not only refers to the words of Jesus (Luke x. 7), but also quotes the precept of Deut. xxv. 4, "Thou shalt not muzzle the ox that treads the corn," and applies it by asking: "Does God care about oxen? Or does he speak thus with us exclusively in view? Of course it was written on our account." Similarly, Philo, in discussing the regulations regarding sacrificial animals, proceeds: "You will discover that all this minuteness in reference to the animal shadows forth by means of symbols the improvement of your character. For the law does not exist for irrational creatures, but for those possessing mind and reason, so that its concern is not for sacrificial animals, to provide that they be without blemish, but for those who offer the sacrifices, that they be not disquieted by reason of any passion." Philo also misses the significance of one of those humane laws

THE OLD TESTAMENT

which characterise the Old Testament code. In Ex. xxii. 26 f. it is said: "If thou take thy neighbour's upper garment as a pledge, thou shalt give it back to him before sunset: for it is his only covering. . . . In what shall he sleep? If he cry to me, I will listen to him, for I am merciful." Philo's comment runs thus: "Is it not meet, if not to reproach, at least to suggest to, those who suppose that the legislator has all this concern about a piece of clothing, What do you mean, my friend, does the Creator and Ruler of the universe call himself merciful in connection with so trifling a matter as the failure of a creditor to return his upper garment to a debtor?' (*De Somn.* i. 92 f.). Strangely enough, Philo expresses his delight in the injunction about oxen, which Paul explains symbolically, and speaks of it as "that tender and gracious ordinance" (*De Virtut.* 145 f.).

The Apostle, however, is extraordinarily sparing in turning history into symbolism. In his treatment of the Old Testament, he often approaches a philosophy of history, as in Gal. iii. 17 ff. But in his doctrine of verbal inspiration he is confronted by the same kind of problem as Philo. For Paul also regards the text of the Old Testament as the literal utterance of God. Like Philo, nevertheless, he does not hesitate, when quoting from the LXX, to omit or supply words for the advantage of his argument: and often, as in his case, Paul's quotations have the inaccuracy which comes from trusting to memory. But his crucial difficulty arises from his attitude towards the Law. *A priori*, the Law, as the revelation of the Divine will, is "holy and righteous and good." It presents an unassailable moral standard. Why, then, has it not satisfied Paul's religious aspirations? At one stage in his career, represented by such passages as Gal. iii. 19, Rom. vii. 13, and Rom. v. 20, he adopts as a working hypothesis the idea that the function of the Law in the purpose of God was to intensify the consciousness of sin, to make the conscience more sensitive to all breaches of the Divine order, and thus to humble

THE OLD TESTAMENT

man as a sinner in presence of the All-holy. But he could not rest there. And in the light of his Christian experience, he feels after a further explanation. Already in Rom. viii. 2 f. he speaks of the Law as baffled by the influence of sinful flesh, human nature as Paul knows it in ordinary experience. Sin, therefore, is to blame for the Law's failure. Yet the admission that human sin so completely foiled what was a Divine method that a new way of salvation had to be brought in, makes clear that Paul was occupying ground which he could not permanently hold. Even in "Galatians," under the pressure of controversy with Judaising Christians, he had ventured to detract from the dignity of the Law, as contrasted with the revelation of grace in Jesus Christ (iii. 19). In the same context, the necessity of a human medium for the legal dispensation, even Moses, constituted for Paul's mind, in diametrical opposition, we may note in passing, to Philo's standpoint, a ground of disparagement. In Gal. iv. 4 and iv. 8–13, he had gone the length of comparing Jewish legalism with pagan ritualism. But in "Colossians," one of his latest Epistles, he takes a more daring step. His growing appreciation of Christ more completely overshadows everything in religion that appears to compete with Him for men's allegiance. And so, in Col. ii. 14 he sternly sweeps away the entire principle of Legalism as something inherently valueless, something whose existence is incompatible with the forgiveness of sin. Thus, as in Philo's case, Paul is driven by the inexorable logic of experience, probably without any formal recognition of what was happening, far away from his original position. He still finds in the Old Testament the revelation of God's will and purpose, but he finds it in such elements as the Divine grace towards Abraham, and the faith of Abraham which responded to it. The later legal aspect of religion stood on a lower plane. It was an "interpolation" (Gal. iii. 19) in the true development.

Before leaving the subject of Philo's relation to the Old Testament *as history*, let us

THE OLD TESTAMENT

note one or two directions in which his method sheds some light on the Fourth Gospel. It is necessary, on the whole, to distinguish between Philo's allegorising and that symbolic element in the Fourth Gospel which comes the more fully to light the more exhaustively its material is investigated. The Evangelist's descriptions of the typical miracles which he selects as "signs," his deliberate association of these with elaborate discussions which aim at a spiritual interpretation of them, his predilection for mysterious sayings which admit of divergent explanations (*e.g.* ii. 19–21, iii. 14–15, iii. 29, iv. 18, iv. 35, vi. 53 f., vii. 38, xii. 24, xiii. 8–10), his use of expressions which have a twofold meaning (i. 30, iii. 3, 8, iii. 14, iv. 10, v. 25, xi. 11, xii. 32, etc.), his symbolic explanations of localities (ix. 7), the inner allusiveness of such passages as i. 46–51, iv. 15–26, etc., his reticence regarding "the disciple whom Jesus loved"—all these phenomena and others of the same kind impart a certain esoteric flavour to the Gospel throughout. That forms an essential element in the author's symbolism. And it involves an elusiveness which marks the contrast with Philo. For in strict allegory, as Mr. J. M. Thompson points out, "a particular" stands for a "particular," whereas "in symbolism proper it stands for something more general than itself."[1] But, of course, the vaguer method often passes into the more detailed correspondence, and *vice versa*. Hence, various points for comparison are obvious. Beside Philo's constant emphasis on the significance of numbers, *e.g.*, on the number 4 (*De Opif. M.* 45–52), on 7 (*ibid.* 89–106), on 10 (*De Decal.* 18–31), may be placed, with some reservation, the six water-pots at Cana, the five husbands of the Samaritan woman, and the five porches at Bethesda. What may be called the "esoteric" element in the vocabulary of the Fourth Gospel, embracing such terms as ὥρα, ἄνωθεν, ὑψωθῆναι, νύμφιος, ὕδωρ ζῶν, οἱ νεκροί, κ.τ.λ., has parallels in Philo's mystic use of τόπος (*De Somn.* ii. 61–68), ἄφεσις

---

[1] *Proceedings of Oxford Society of Historical Theology*, Dec. 4, 1913, p. 25.

THE OLD TESTAMENT

(*De Migr. Abr.* 32), and πηγή (*De Fuga*, 177 f.). Only, Philo expounds the meaning of these words, while the Evangelist seems to count upon an understanding of his terms in the circle for which he writes. Specially noteworthy in Philo is his elaborate symbolism of names. Names and their component parts, he says (*De Mutat. Nom.* 65), are really "distinctive marks of capacities" (χαρακτῆρες δυνάμεων), and, on this principle, such proper names as Egypt, Joseph, Leah, Rachel, etc., designate certain definite qualities or characters. The interpretation of Siloam by the Evangelist suggests an allied standpoint, and possibly, if we had a clue to the usage of his circle, the same might be said of such names as Nathanael and Nicodemus. Curiously enough, Philo shows the same kind of reticence about Jacob's son, Judah, whom he usually describes as "the fourth in age" (e.g. *De Joseph.* 15, 189) without mentioning him by name, as the Fourth Evangelist with regard to "the disciple whom Jesus loved."

We enter a less obscure region when we

try to estimate the discourses of the Fourth Gospel in the light of Philo's practice. Indeed, the latter gives us a most arresting clue to the attitude of ancient thinkers towards that which they reckoned to be history. We know that for him the Pentateuch was inspired in every detail. Yet in narrating, *e.g.*, God's instructions to Moses to warn Pharaoh, as reported in Ex. iv. 11 f., he expands the discourse on lines of his own, simply making the original his starting-point (*De Vita M.* i. 84). Even more remarkable is his recasting and elaboration of Moses' injunctions to the spies before they left on their errand (*ibid.* 222–226). Taking Num. xiii. 17–20 as his basis, he constructs upon it a composition which embodies some of its leading ideas, but supplements them in every direction.[1] This process illustrates the usage of the Fourth Evangelist, for whom some saying or thought of Jesus forms the text of a carefully articulated

---

[1] Perhaps Philo was here indebted to the tradition of the πρεσβύτεροι: see *Vita M.* i. 4, referred to by Schürer, *H.J.P.*, Div. ii. vol. iii. p. 365.

THE OLD TESTAMENT

discourse. It appears to him in no sense arbitrary to draw out on these lines the significance of a message which he regarded as wholly Divine.

We have still to deal with Philo's relation to the Law, as such, a subject which can only be sketched in outline. The main task he prescribed for himself was to expound the Pentateuch in its most universal bearings. For he regards Moses as the incomparable legislator for humanity. "His laws alone, stable, unshaken, undisturbed, bearing the impress of the seal of Nature herself, remain firm from the day when they were written until now, and, we trust, will abide for all time coming, endowed with immortality, as long as sun and moon and the entire heavens and universe endure" (*De Vita M.* ii. 14). For this reason their scope reaches far beyond national limits. And Philo's aim is to show that they enshrine all that is of value in pagan philosophy. His method, of course, supplies the instrument for that purpose. But over and above the results reached by the use of allegory, Philo deliberately emphasises the complete harmony of the Mosaic Law with the Law of Nature. He was deeply imbued with that Stoic doctrine, and at the very opening of his great allegorical commentary on the Pentateuch he strikes this note: "This beginning (*i.e.* this book of Genesis) is . . . worthy of the highest admiration, as it contains a description of the creation of the world, to show that the world is in harmony with the law, as the law is with the world, and that the man who obeys the law is for that reason a citizen of the world, since he guides his activities according to the will of Nature (πρὸς τὸ βούλημα τῆς φύσεως), by which the entire universe is directed" (*De Opif. Mund.* 3). Here is the famous Stoic maxim, "to live in harmony with Nature," set in the forefront of his enterprise. We are therefore not surprised to find in his more detailed account of the Mosaic legislation that Moses "began with the creation of the universe, in order to set forth his most necessary doctrines, first, that the Father and Creator of the world is the same as the real legislator; and second, that

THE OLD TESTAMENT

he who is willing to live by these laws will gladly strive after harmony with Nature, and will live in accordance with the ordinances of the universe, bringing his words into agreement with his deeds, and his deeds with his words" (*De Vita Mos.* ii. 48).[1] But a position like this has far-reaching implications. Hence Drummond is probably justified in saying that for Philo "the Pentateuch was simply the Divine Logos resolved into Logoi, statements of philosophical truth, and precepts of the moral code" (*Philo Judaeus*, ii. p. 308).

When such a point is reached, we are prepared for the conception of Conscience, the legislative Reason within us, which is one of Philo's most remarkable contributions to the content of ancient ethics. Also, we

[1] Bréhier points out an interesting affinity in this connection between Philo and Cicero (*De Republica* and *De Legibus*): "They show a similar anxiety to champion their respective laws by placing them under the aegis of Natural Law" (*Les Idées Philosophiques et Religieuses de Philon*, p. 12). He does not mention that these works of Cicero have as their main source the Stoic teacher Panaetius (see Schmekel, *Die Mittlere Stoa*, pp. 47–63, 67–85). Philo constantly reveals the influence of Posidonius, the pupil of Panaetius.

are in no way surprised to find that Philo transfers the emphasis from the ritual of the Law to the condition of the soul before God. "Let me tell you, my friend," he declares, "that God feels no joy when we bring him hecatombs, for all things are his possession. . . . But he delights in pious dispositions and in men who practise holiness, and from them he gladly receives sacrificial cakes and grains of barley and the most frugal offerings as of highest worth. . . . And even though they bring nothing else, in bringing themselves, the most perfect completion of noble character, they present the best sacrifice, honouring God their Benefactor and Saviour with hymns and thanksgivings" (*De Spec. Leg.* i. 271 f.). But, as Bréhier points out, "this inward morality is not purely and simply morality, it is morality accompanied by the consciousness of its superhuman, Divine origin" (*op. cit.* p. 228). Plainly, such a process throws the door wide open for that universal validity of the Law so dear to the mind of Philo. He appears to be conscious of occupying a unique position. "We instruct

THE OLD TESTAMENT

in the Divine mysteries those initiates who are worthy of the most sacred ritual: these are the people who, without arrogance, practise true and genuinely unadorned piety, but we shall never be hierophants for those in the grasp of an incurable disease, the stupidity of set phrases, the paltry trifling with names, the clap-trap of appointed customs" (*De Cherub.* 42). The statement quoted earlier from *De Migr. Abr.* 89 as emphasising adherence to the strict letter of the law, though apparently a direct contradiction of this, is really modified by what immediately follows it. "As it is," he says, "like people living alone in isolation or bodiless souls, having no communication with city or village or family or any human company, they look down upon the opinion of the multitude, and search for bare truth in itself: and yet the sacred word teaches them to pay respect to estimable public opinion and to abolish none of those usages established by inspired men who surpassed any of our time. . . . It is the part of the mature soul to share both in being and in seeming to be : it must aim not only at gaining esteem in the men's quarters, but also at being praised at the hearth where the women sit" (*ibid.* 90, 96). Thus, one element, at least, in Philo's concern for observance of the *letter* of the law springs from the fear of wounding the consciences of others, although in certain moods he can speak of such "weak" brethren in a tone of disparagement.

It is worth observing how, along a very divergent line of development, Philo arrives at a position regarding the Law which approximates to that of Paul. His religious instinct, as well as the spiritual atmosphere in which he moves, leads him away from the region of ceremonial into that of obedience to the Divine will, whose appeal he hears within. The Christian Apostle, with surer spiritual vision, discovers through his crucial experience of Christ a Divine Love which seeks him out and to which his soul can make answer with adoring gratitude. This heartfelt devotion takes the place of legal obedience. But each, in his own manner, has come to realise the accomplishment of Jere-

THE OLD TESTAMENT

miah's epoch-making utterance: " I will put my law in their inward parts, and write it in their hearts " (xxxi. 33).

This quotation suggests a reference to Philo's attitude towards the Prophets. We have already seen that for him Moses stands supreme above all the rest. And that is borne out by the solitary level on which he places the Pentateuch. Indeed, if we were content to apply the rough and ready test of quotation, this subject might be dismissed without more ado. For in Dr. Ryle's classification of the material, six pages of extracts represent the Old Testament prophets as against two hundred and eighty-eight for the Pentateuch. Windisch goes the length of saying that Philo was scarcely influenced by them at all (*Die Frömmigkeit Philos*, p. 93). We are rather inclined to apply to them what Windisch himself says, in the same connection, of the Psalms, that they affected Philo more powerfully than he acknowledges (*op. cit.* p. 94). It is true and surprising that he has not attempted to allegorise the prophetic writings, when we remember how current this practice was among the Fathers of the early Church.[1] Possibly one reason may have been that his interest did not lie in history, not even in the historical experiences of his own nation. And it would have been difficult to offer any kind of exposition of these glowing utterances, apart from an earnest participation in the Hope which pervaded them, or at least in the expectation of those great eschatological events which loomed before their minds. We know that Paul, as a Christian, rediscovered the prophets, as Jesus had done, and carried their lofty spiritual intuitions into the life and thought of the new community. Philo, in his own special environment, and on the path of his own religious development, at least reflects some of the most vital of the prophetic achievements. The primacy which he assigns to the inward worship of the spirit over all sacrificial rites places us at the heart of the religion of the prophets. It is quite possible, as Bréhier suggests (*op. cit.* p. 227), that his distance from Jerusalem and its Temple, and

---

[1] See, *e.g.*, Hatch, *Influence of Greek Ideas on Christianity*, pp. 72, 73.

THE OLD TESTAMENT

his association of worship with the Synagogue, in part account for this affinity. To us it appears that the clue lies deeper. We are not even inclined to lay strong emphasis on his familiarity with an idealistic type of philosophy which discountenanced anthropomorphism. Must not his receptiveness towards the spiritual have been one of the main factors in creating his philosophic interest? Is it not rather his view of God, and of the grace of God, and of God's interest in man, which reminds us over and over again of Hosea and Isaiah? And does not this go back to a personal religious experience, similar in kind to that in which the prophets became profoundly aware of God?

CHAPTER III

FUNDAMENTAL PROBLEMS

THE career of Philo belongs to a period notable for its philosophical syncretism, and his own position in philosophy is one of the most characteristic products of his age. It is, as we shall have occasion to note, a blending of theories belonging to various schools, and probably for that reason he found it easier to insert within its framework much of his inherited Judaism. The outcome of such a process could never take shape as a coherent system, and Philo's scheme of thought reveals ragged edges on every side.

The question has been keenly discussed whether Philo himself is directly responsible for this remarkable synthesis of Platonic and Stoic doctrine, powerfully coloured by Pythagorean tradition, or whether, as Schmekel

FUNDAMENTAL PROBLEMS

(*Die Mittlere Stoa*, pp. 409 ff., 428 ff.) and others believe, he was predominantly influenced by Posidonius, and especially by the famous commentary of the latter on Plato's *Timaeus*, an exposition which left its mark on numerous writers of that epoch. The question is really secondary. For it is universally admitted that Posidonius, to a unique extent, summed up in himself the eclectic tendencies of the time. There can be little doubt that Philo was acquainted with his works, but he must also have come into contact with similar currents of thought throughout his environment, and in all likelihood he himself contributed more or less to the syncretistic process.[1]

At every turn his allegorical exposition of the Law contains discussions of problems which did not present themselves even to serious Jewish thinkers. Yet in his attempts to solve these problems, moulded as they are by Platonic-Stoic speculations, we can

[1] Cf. the important evidence for Philo's affinities with the Hermetic documents in J. Kroll's *Die Lehren d. Hermes Trismegistos*, Münster i. W., 1914.

frequently discern, from the points where he places the emphasis or the directions in which he leads the argument, the effect of his training in the Old Testament and the pressure of certain inviolable religious postulates.

(a) *God and the World*

No more searching criterion can be applied to the structure of Philo's philosophy, with a view to discovering the relation of his adopted metaphysics to his ancestral and still living faith, than an examination of his attitude towards the perennial *crux* for ancient thought, the connection between Spirit and Matter, between God and the World. This, it need scarcely be said, was not a problem for Old Testament religion. Even in the Wisdom-sections of *Proverbs* there is no more than a suggestion of the metaphysical. The precise relations of the personified Wisdom to God and the World are in no sense investigated. We find little cogency in Siegfried's arguments (*Philo von Alexandria*, p. 230 f.) for his assertion that Philo's cosmogony was based on current Jewish expositions of the work of

FUNDAMENTAL PROBLEMS

creation. Its main source, whether used directly or through such a medium as Posidonius' commentary, seems to be Plato's *Timaeus*,[1] modified by an adaptation of the Stoic conception of God and considerably affected by Jewish presuppositions.

Let us briefly consider the facts. "Moses," says Philo (*De Opif. Mundi*, 8 f.), "who had reached the summit of philosophy and had received instruction by Divine revelation concerning the most important aspects of Nature, recognised that among existing things there must be, on the one hand, an active Cause (δραστήριον αἴτιον), on the other a passive (παθητόν), and that the active is the mind (νοῦς) of the universe, perfectly pure and unmixed, better than knowledge, better than the good in itself and the beautiful in itself, while the passive has no life (ἄψυχον) and is motionless of itself, but when moved and shaped and quickened by mind becomes transformed into the most perfect product, this

---

[1] Mr. Barker points out (*Greek Political Theory*, p. 352, note 2) that the Mediæval period "drew its cosmology largely" from the *Timaeus*, "which . . . was practically the only work of Plato known directly to the Middle Ages."

universe of ours." Here we are on familiar Stoic ground,[1] and perhaps this group of ideas has influenced Philo more powerfully than scholars have usually imagined. Some passages which follow point in another direction. "The great Moses," he proceeds, "regarding that which had no becoming as alien to the visible, ascribed to the invisible which can only be conceived (νοητόν), as its most appropriate attribute, eternity, but to that which was perceivable by the senses, as its befitting name genesis" (becoming). This is, of course, the Platonic distinction between the real and the phenomenal. But how are these contrasted magnitudes, the Active and the Passive, the Eternal and that which comes into being, related? Philo grapples with the question as follows: "Since God in virtue of his Deity realised beforehand that a beautiful copy (μίμημα) could not come into being apart from a beautiful pattern (παραδείγματος), and that none of the things perceived by sense could be flawless which was not made after the image (ἀπεικονίσθη) of an Archetype and a spiritual

[1] See esp. *Diog. Laert.* vii. 134 ; Seneca, *Ep.* lxv. 2.

FUNDAMENTAL PROBLEMS

(νοητήν) Idea, when he designed to create this visible world, he first formed the ideal world, so that he might produce the bodily by the use of an incorporeal and most Godlike pattern, the later modelled on the earlier, and intended to contain as many classes of things (γένη) apprehensible by the senses as there were ideas in the archetypal world" (*op. cit.* 16). This is perhaps his clearest description of the Divine plan in creation, and it reflects Plato's argument in *Timaeus*, 28 A, B, 29 A. But there is no mention in it of Matter. We mainly gather from it the high value Philo assigned to the notion of an archetypal world in the process of creation.

Similarly, his conception of the motive of creation closely follows *Timaeus*, 29 E, 30 A, B. " If any one should desire to investigate the reason why this universe was created, I should think he would not be far from the mark in saying, as indeed one of the ancients (*i.e.* Plato) has said, that the Father and Maker of all things is gracious. On this account he did not grudge his perfect nature to matter (οὐσίᾳ), which possesses nothing

FUNDAMENTAL PROBLEMS

beautiful of itself but has the capacity of becoming all things" (*op. cit.* 21). In taking up what is for the Plato of the *Timaeus* a semi-mythical standpoint, Philo was really true to his inherited and most real faith in a good and gracious God, who was the Source of all being and the Giver of nothing but benefits to His creatures, and whose peculiar characteristic is, he affirms, to create (*Leg. All.* i. 5). But how did this plan, the outcome of a beneficent purpose, actually work? Did God create out of nothing? What place and meaning does Philo assign to the Matter (οὐσία) of which he speaks? "It was unordered of itself, devoid of qualities, without life,[1] abounding in difference, disagreement, discord. But it received a change and transformation into what was opposite and best, order, quality, vitality, likeness, identity, concord, harmony, all the attributes of the higher Idea " (*op. cit.* 22). Again, in commenting on Gen. i. 31, "God saw all that he had created, and behold it was very good," he observes: "God did not praise the matter (ὕλην)

[1] Omitting ἀνόμοιος, conjectured by Markland.

FUNDAMENTAL PROBLEMS

which he had used for creation, lifeless and discordant and dissoluble and, moreover, perishable of itself and irregular and unequal, but he praised the products of his own skill, finished according to a single equal and regular power" (*Quis Rer. Div. H.* 160). And once more: "That opinion which does away with Ideas confuses everything and refers it to the ultimate matter (οὐσία) of the elements which is without form and quality. But what could be more absurd? for it was out of that that God produced all things, not touching it himself—for it was not fitting that the happy and blessed One should touch undefined and confused matter (ὕλης)—but he used those incorporeal forms, whose proper name is the Ideas, in order that each class of things should receive its suitable shape" (*De Spec. Leg.* i. 328 f.).

In these passages he seems to use οὐσία or ὕλη without distinction for Matter, and to regard it as in some sense existing independently of God. It is there in its passivity, awaiting the action of the Divine Artificer. It is lifeless and without qualities, confused and

FUNDAMENTAL PROBLEMS

chaotic. It has to receive the impress of the ideal Forms, which Philo seems to identify with the λόγοι of the Stoics, and which proceed from the Divine mind and are its expressed thoughts, operating upon this undefined material. Thus it becomes Cosmos, the ordered universe.

Did Philo, then, regard Matter as eternally there? Such a position would, of course, be in absolute conflict with Jewish conceptions. And it is possible to quote a statement which appears to contradict what has been said above, *De Somn.* i. 76: "As the sun, when it has risen, reveals the hidden parts of bodies, so also God, who begat all things, not only brought them to light, but also created what before was not in existence, since he was not only artificer (δημιουργός) but also creator (κτίστης)." It is true that Matter is not distinctly mentioned, but surely the sharp antithesis between δημιουργός, the word he regularly uses for the shaping of chaos into cosmos, and κτίστης, Creator in the strict sense, suggests that here he occupies the position which appealed to a devout Jew,

FUNDAMENTAL PROBLEMS

that nothing came into being without God. Further, his description of Matter in *Quis Rer. Div. H.* 160, already quoted, as "perishable of itself" seems to preclude a distinct hypothesis of pre-existence.[1] The discrepancy[2] between this and the statements cited above is not surprising in so eclectic a thinker. We may even venture to doubt whether Philo ever faced the problem of the eternity of matter. There is no direct hint of it in his writings. What concerned him was God's creative efficacy, and probably he was content to assume a formless, lifeless substratum of things, somehow available to receive the Divine impress. Possibly, in his

---

[1] Drummond's attempt (*Philo Judaeus*, i. p. 301 f.) to prove that here "it is not matter, but 'fabricated matter,' which is said to be thus corruptible," seems to us to be based on a misinterpretation of Philo's language, for the adjectives he attaches to ὕλην, which are of precisely the same type as he applies to ὕλη or οὐσία in the other quotations given plainly qualify ὕλην itself, and not the compound expression δημιουργηθεῖσαν ὕλην. After it has been used for creation (δημιουργηθεῖσα), *i.e.* according to Philo, "changed into what was best" under the operation of the Divine Ideas, Matter can no longer be called "lifeless, discordant, dissoluble perishable of itself," as here.

[2] Heinze, in his learned treatise, *Die Lehre vom Logos* p. 210, note, takes the same view.

descriptions of ὕλη or οὐσία he is influenced by such statements as that of *Timaeus*, 51 A: "The mother and recipient (ὑποδοχή) of created things which are visible and by any sense perceptible we must call neither earth nor air nor fire nor water ... but we shall not err in affirming it to be a kind of invisible and formless being (εἶδός τι), all-receiving, in some manner most bewildering and hard to understand, partaking of the intelligible." This ὑποδοχή Plato identifies in *Tim*. 52 A, B with empty Space (see Zeller, *Plato*, p. 304 ff.). It is not a "substance" posited beside the Ideas and the phenomenal world. It is for him non-being. This modification of an absolute Dualism is, we think, confirmed by Philo's view of the character of Matter. We have referred more than once to the epithets he applies to it. These are practically all of a negative kind, "unordered, devoid of qualities, without life, abounding in difference," and the like. In other words, he regards it as the formless substratum of created things, in itself wholly "passive." Yet it has " the capacity of becoming all things."

FUNDAMENTAL PROBLEMS

Is it legitimate to say, as Siegfried (*op. cit.* p. 232) and other scholars do, that for Philo Matter is evil? Siegfried's argument is quite unconvincing. It is derived from the comment on Gen. i. 31, quoted above, that " God did not praise the matter used by him in creation . . . but praised the products of his skill." The inference goes far beyond the data. Matter as " devoid of qualities" lies outside the realm of approval or disapproval. It is necessarily something indifferent, a mere potentiality, which attains positive value only when it is transformed through the influence of "the higher Idea" into " quality, vitality, identity," *i.e.* into "a product of the Divine skill." We can find no trace in Philo of any active function being ascribed to Matter, not even resistance to the transforming energy of the Artificer as mediated by His "powers." For the notion of a restriction of God's creative operations he does not associate with Matter, as Drummond relevantly notes (*op. cit.* i. p. 311), but with that which has come into being (γένεσις) in the strict sense. " Not according to the magnitude of his gracious thoughts—for that is without limit or end—does he show forth his benefits, but according to the capacities of those who are benefited. For not according to God's power of conferring good is that of the created thing (τὸ γενόμενον) to receive it. For God's capacities cannot be measured; but the created thing, being too weak to receive the magnitude of them, would have failed, had not God calculated and fittingly measured out to each that which was its portion" (*De Op. M.* 23). The conception appears in various passages, perhaps most strikingly in *De Vita Mos.* ii. (iii.) 147, where, in speaking of the calf offered as a sin-offering, he finds in this a symbol that "sin is innate in every one born (παντὶ γενητῷ), even if he be virtuous, by reason of his coming to birth" (εἰς γένεσιν). Nothing like this is ever said about Matter. Plato, we know, regards the phenomenal as imperfect because there belongs to it not only the existence imparted by the Idea, but that also which makes it a phenomenon and to that extent limits the Idea. Philo follows his master in recognising

FUNDAMENTAL PROBLEMS

that the phenomenon is separated by a vast chasm from the Creator. One important passage recalls Plato's belief that "the generation (γένεσις) of this universe was a mixed creation by a combination of necessity (ἀναγκή) and reason" (*Tim.* 48 A).[1] " God alone," Philo says, " is most true and genuine peace, but all matter (οὐσία), as having come into being (γενητή) and perishable (φθαρτή), is constant warfare. For God is free activity, while matter is necessity. Whosoever, therefore, is able to leave behind warfare and necessity and becoming and decay, and to take refuge with that which has no becoming or decay, free activity, peace, might rightly be called the dwelling-place and city of God " (*De Somn.* ii. 353). Here he recognises, without discussion, the fact of an inner necessity in created things, which sets them in contrast with the freedom of God. But this necessity is not the mark of an absolute dualism. It is inseparable, as in Plato, from

[1] Archer Hind here interprets ἀναγκή as " the laws which govern the existence of νοῦς in the form of plurality." This exposition opens up a peculiarly fascinating vista of speculation.

the entrance of Eternal Being, however mediated, into the realm of the visible. Thus the stamp of imperfection, from the nature of the case, lies upon the phenomenon. But that is far from the position that Matter is evil, a position which to a thinker who conceived God as Philo did would have seemed profane.

It may be said, then, that we find no perfectly clear conception of Matter in Philo. Sometimes he seems to approach Plato's notion of Non-Being; at others we are reminded of the Stoic conception of Active and Passive as expressing modes of a single substance, which can be separated in thought, though not in fact, denoting at the one extreme the highest Divine mind, at the other the most indeterminate form of Matter: while some passages cannot be fairly interpreted without ascribing Matter to the creative energy of God. But there is nothing to show that Philo regarded Matter *per se* as evil. This fact is important for its bearing on the significance of the Pauline antithesis between Flesh and Spirit, which meets us in the next phase of our discussion.

FUNDAMENTAL PROBLEMS

(b) *The Constitution of Human Nature*

Man is for Philo the crowning example of the entrance of Spirit or Mind into a material environment. And he describes both the process and its consequences in an endless variety of ways. Fundamentally, man consists of soul (ψυχή) and body (σῶμα). "There are two elements," he says (*Leg. Alleg.* iii. 161), "of which we are composed, namely, soul and body: the body has been fashioned of earth, but the soul belongs to the ether, a fragment of the Divine: for 'God breathed into his face the breath (πνεῦμα) of life, so that man became a living soul'" (Gen. ii. 7). Or, stated more philosophically: "Man is the noblest of animals, by reason of the higher element among his component parts, the soul, closely akin to heaven, which is most pure in its essence, and to the Father of the universe, as having received mind (νοῦν), of all things on earth the most faithful image and copy of the eternal and blessed Idea" (*De Decal.* 134). Equally important for Philo is this religious

FUNDAMENTAL PROBLEMS

definition: "It is written in the book of God that man alone is full of good hope.... Hence the definition of us men as a compound is a rational, mortal animal. But that of man according to Moses is a condition of soul which sets its hope on the truly existent God" (*Quod det. pot.* 139).

Repeatedly Philo indulges in a speculation which must have fascinated him, dealing with a twofold creation of man, based upon (1) Gen. i. 27: "God made (ἐποίησεν) man, after the image (εἰκόνα) of God he made him," and (2) Gen. ii. 7: "God formed (ἔπλασεν) man of dust from the earth, and breathed," etc. We refer to it here as a remarkable instance of his attempt to combine the influence of Greek metaphysics with that of Hebrew tradition. Having quoted Gen. ii. 7, he continues (*De Op. Mund.* 134 f.): "Most clearly does he show by this that there is an immense difference between the man now formed (πλασθέντος) and him who had earlier come into being (γεγονότος) according to the image of God. For the man now formed was perceptible by sense (αἰσθητός),

FUNDAMENTAL PROBLEMS

already participating in quality, composed of body and soul, man or woman, mortal by nature; while he who was made after the Divine image was a sort of idea (ἰδέα τις) or class or soul, apprehensible only by thought, incorporeal, neither male nor female, immortal by nature. Moreover, he says that the constitution of the individual man, perceptible by sense, was composed of earthly substance and the Divine breath (πνεύματος). For what he breathed into him was nothing else than a Divine breath (or, spirit) which took its departure hither from that blessed and happy nature for the good of our race. So that if it is mortal so far as its visible part is concerned, as regards its invisible part at least it possesses immortality."[1]

Bousset and others have tried to link on

[1] Bréhier (*op. cit.* p. 121 f.) seems to us completely mistaken in his interpretation of *De Op. M.* 69, in which he tries to show that that passage refers to the Divine Man, but contradicts the view in *De Op. M.* 134 f., and *Leg. Alleg.* i. 31 ff. For in the first passage, although Philo refers to Gen. i. 26, he has not before his mind the contrast between the ideal and the earth-born man at all. He is thinking only of the latter, as the statement, "for nothing earth-born is more like to God than man," clearly indicates. And so he explains the εἰκὼν θεοῦ as referring to man's νοῦς.

Philo's ideal man to the early myth of an Ur-Anthropos, of which they find traces in various Gnostic documents. The hypothesis is unnecessary, for the Ideal Man is postulated by Philo's Platonic theory already described, of God's method in the creation of the visible world, according to which things perceived by sense require a perfect pattern of which they are copies. The slightest examination of the data suffices to show the irrelevance of the attempt made by some scholars to explain from this notion of a twofold creation Paul's statement as to the "first man Adam" and the "last Adam," the "earthly" ($\chi o\ddot{\iota}\kappa\acute{o}\varsigma$) and the "heavenly" ($\dot{\epsilon}\pi o \nu \rho \acute{a} \nu \iota o \varsigma$). The very fact that Paul calls the "earthly" the "first man," and the "heavenly" the "second man," while the whole point of Philo's argument turns on the priority of the ideal man, is decisive. It is true that the Apostle describes Christ as "the image of the invisible God, the first-begotten of all creation" (Col. i. 15); but the remarkable words which follow: "for in him were created all things in heaven and on earth, the

FUNDAMENTAL PROBLEMS

visible and the invisible, . . . and he is before all things and in him all things cohere " (i. 16 f.), have an immensely wider scope than Philo's conception of the ideal man. If we wish, therefore, to compare St. Paul's cosmological doctrines with those of Philo, this famous passage points in the direction of the Logos, the central principle which unifies the cosmos : e.g. *De Somn.* ii. 45 : "God . . . sealed the universe with an image and idea, his own Logos."

The speculation to which we have just referred is, in a sense, typical of Philo's views on the origin and constitution of human nature. These often consist of an attempted blend of Platonic, Stoic, and Aristotelian conceptions. Often they represent Philo's theological bias, to a large extent moulded by Old Testament ideas. In the latter case, he does not hesitate to assume an unmediated influence of God on human nature, a position at variance with his philosophical theories, which demand the employment of mediating forces to bring together the Infinite and the finite. The

FUNDAMENTAL PROBLEMS

influence of the *Timaeus* accounts for one of his most discordant hypotheses, that of the pre-existence of souls in the air. In the semi-mythical tone characteristic of that dialogue, Plato describes (*Tim.* 41 D–43 A, 69 A–70 A) how the Creator entrusted to the "young gods" the confining of souls who had previously formed part of the universal Soul in mortal bodies. Philo (esp. *De Gig.* 6–15) depicts in his fanciful narrative the fortunes of these souls, who, somehow, stooped from their pure dwelling in the air to incarnation in mortal bodies, leaving behind them an incorruptible group of fellow-souls, whom God used as His ministers for the supervision of mortals, and whom Moses called "angels." Of those incarnate, some were able to resist the current of sensuous life and to return to their original abode; the others, surrendering themselves to restless activities, were engulfed in the illusory world of wealth, fame and similar unreal things. Some scholars, *e.g.* Zeller (*Phil. d. Griechen*[4], 3te Theil, 2te Hälfte, p. 450 f.), refer Philo's entire conception

FUNDAMENTAL PROBLEMS

of human sin to this hypothesis. In our judgment it seems to be largely a side-issue. And it is far more rewarding to follow the main trend of his ideas, recognising throughout that these cannot be adjusted in a coherent system.

No more comprehensive passage could be selected for our purpose than *Quod det. pot. insid. sol.* 82–90. "It follows," he says, "from our recent analysis, that each of us is numerically two, an animal and a man: to each of these has been assigned its proper spiritual potency, to the one that vital principle (ἡ ζωτική) by which we live, to the other the rational (ἡ λογική) in virtue of which we are rational. In the vital principle material things also share, but in the rational God does not share: he is its source, the fountain of the primal reason (λόγος). To that potency, then, which we share with irrational things, blood was assigned as its substance (οὐσία), but that derived from the rational principle had for its essence spirit (or, breath, πνεῦμα), not air set in motion, but a sort of stamp and impress of the Divine

FUNDAMENTAL PROBLEMS

power, which Moses calls by its proper name, image (εἰκών), showing that God is the archetype of the rational nature, and man its copy and facsimile, not the animal of twofold nature, but the noblest aspect (εἶδος)[1] of the soul, which is called mind (νοῦς) and reason (λόγος). On this account he makes blood the soul of the flesh, recognising that the fleshly nature (ἡ σαρκὸς φύσις) has no part in mind, but partakes of life just like our whole body. But the soul of man he names spirit (πνεῦμα), designating as man not the compound, as I said, but that Godlike product of creation by which we reason, whose roots he stretched to heaven. . . . For alone of earthly creatures, God made man a heavenly plant, bending the head of the others towards the ground . . . but making man look upwards. . . . Let us therefore, who are disciples of Moses, be in no doubt as to how man received his conception (ἔννοιαν) of the unseen God. . . . Here are his (*i.e.* Moses') words: 'The

---

[1] It is impossible to find a thoroughly satisfactory rendering of εἶδος here. It means something more fundamental than "aspect" in its ordinary sense. Perhaps "quality" might serve.

FUNDAMENTAL PROBLEMS

Maker prepared for the body no soul sufficient of itself to see its maker, but, considering the great benefit of the creation, if it might receive a conception of its Creator . . . he breathed into it from above of his own divinity.' . . . How, then, is it likely that so restricted a thing as the human mind . . . should have room for the vastness of heaven and the world if it were not an undivided portion of that divine and blessed Spirit (ψυχῆς)? For no part of the Divine is separated by detachment, it is only an extension of it."

Perhaps this statement may reflect the theological more than the philosophical aspect of Philo's thought, but that accords with his bent, and reminds us that his Old Testament training remained fundamental for his entire speculation. The passage reveals his essential view of human nature, the supreme distinction between the rational and the irrational in man. Before we examine these two elements more closely, let us make clear a point which has only been hinted at in the quotation. "For the con-

FUNDAMENTAL PROBLEMS

stituting of the soul," he observes, "God seems to have used as pattern no created thing, but only . . . his own Logos. Of this, therefore, . . . man was made the facsimile and copy, for his face was breathed into, that part which is the seat of the senses with which the Creator vitalised (ἐψύχωσεν) the body: but having implanted the reason as ruler, he handed over the senses to this governing element, so as to have them at its service for the apprehension of colours, sounds, tastes, odours and the like, which, by itself alone, apart from sense-perception, it would have been unable to grasp" (*De Op. M*. 139). To realise the fluidity of Philo's conceptions, we may compare with this *Leg. Alleg*. i. 37: God is the in-breathing force, that which receives his breath is the reason (or, mind, νοῦς), that which is inbreathed is the spirit (πνεῦμα). . . . God breathes into this (*i.e.* νοῦς) alone, but the other parts he does not think worthy of such action, I mean, the senses and the faculties of speech and reproduction, for they are secondary in their capacity. By what,

FUNDAMENTAL PROBLEMS

then, did these receive (vital) breath? Plainly by reason ($νοῦς$), for that in which God enabled reason to share, it imparted to the irrational element of the soul, so that reason was vitalised by God, and the material element by reason." Here he presupposes a human reason, which receives Divine influence, and transmits it for the establishing of sense-life; whereas, in the former passage, sense-life had already been constituted by God, and awaited the inbreaking of a higher energy, reason itself. A similar oscillation of ideas is found regarding the function of the Logos in creation. Commenting, as so frequently, on Gen. i. 26, he says: "The Father of the universe converses with his own powers, to whom he assigned the fashioning of the mortal part of the soul, who copied his skill when he shaped the rational element in us, judging it right that the dominating principle in the soul should be created by the Ruler, but the subordinate by his subordinates" (*De Fuga*, 69 f.). The latter creation he calls in the next sentence τὴν κακῶν γένεσιν, the former,

FUNDAMENTAL PROBLEMS

τὴν τῶν ἀγαθῶν. Here is a curious parallel to the "young gods" of the *Timaeus*; but the idea, of course, tallies both with Stoic and even Jewish conceptions of mediation between the Infinite and the finite.

In the passages quoted above we have a rough summary of Philo's conception of the Constitution of Human Nature. The body (σῶμα), which has been moulded by the Divine power,[1] is animated by the soul (ψυχή), which, however, has to be viewed under two contrasted aspects. To it belongs the vital energy (ἡ ζωτικὴ δύναμις, where ζ. = Paul's adjective, ψυχικός), the principle of life in matter, irrational and common to us with

---

[1] Curiously enough, there are exceeding few references n Philo to the formation of the σῶμα by God, and these are incidental: e.g. *Quis Rer. Div. H.* 73: θεῷ τῷ καὶ τὸ σῶμα σωματοῦντι καὶ πηγνύντι; *Leg. Alleg.* iii. 73: ἵνα εἴδῃς ὅτι καὶ τὰ ἄψυχα οὐκ ἐξουσίᾳ πεποίηκεν, ἀλλ' ἀγαθότητι, ᾗ καὶ τὰ ἔμψυχα. Probably this is due to his fundamental notion of the transiency of the body, and the inferiority which thus characterises it. In a striking passage he represents the elements, earth and water, as saying: "We are the matter of your body: Nature having mixed us, shaped us by her divine art into the semblance of the human form" (*De Spec. Leg.* i. 266). The moulding of the body is here ascribed to Φύσις, almost as if he wished to avoid connecting the process with God.

FUNDAMENTAL PROBLEMS

other animals. The essence of this vital principle is blood. Here he is strictly loyal to Hebrew ideas; *e.g.* Lev. xvii. 11 (LXX): "for the soul (ψυχή) of all flesh (σαρκός) is its blood." On the other hand, it possesses a rational capacity which links it to God, that being the image or impress of the Divine reason. Pictorially, this higher element is described as breathed into man by God. As such it is called "spirit" or "breath" (πνεῦμα).[1] But it may also be named νοῦς or λόγος, for it is really an undivided part of the Divine Reason (λόγος). As such it is the medium by which we reach a conception of the unseen God. No doubt Philo found it easier to conceive this ultimate relation between the finite and the Infinite, because he had already posited the Divine Logos as God's instrument in creation, God's reason operating in the cosmos almost as a personal mediator. Occasionally he seems to presuppose a human νοῦς, whose origin he does not explain, which is the receptacle

---

[1] See esp. *De Spec. Leg.* iv. 123, where blood=οὐσία ψυχῆς αἰσθητικῆς, while Divine Spirit=οὐσία ψυχῆς νοερᾶς.

FUNDAMENTAL PROBLEMS

of higher Divine influence, and in which the senses, elsewhere ascribed to the direct action of the Creator upon the body, find their vitality. In any case, the life of sense (αἴσθησις), according to the Divine intention, is subordinated to the dominant power (τὸ ἡγεμονικόν), a synonym for reason in its highest capacity, and is sometimes attributed to the action of the subordinate "powers" (δυνάμεις) of God.

Let us briefly examine the chief elements into which Philo analyses human nature, keeping in view their relation to parallel phenomena in the New Testament. The body (σῶμα) is regularly described as fashioned from earth (e.g. *Leg. Alleg.* iii. 161), and as such is, of course, inferior to the reason which informs it. It is peculiarly the basis of the sense-life (e.g. *Quod det. pot.* 109) and of the passions (e.g. *Quis Rer. Div. D.* 268 : " Alien to the understanding are the passions, which belong truly to the body, springing out of the flesh in which they have their roots "). Since the desires which are fostered by the senses and the force of the passions, as a matter of experience, war against the higher aspirations

FUNDAMENTAL PROBLEMS

of the rational element in the soul, Philo constantly identifies himself with the Neo-Pythagorean position that the body is the source of evil. "Away, my friend," he exclaims, "from that earthly vesture of yours, escape from that accursed prison, the body, and from its pleasures and lusts, which are your jailors" (*De. Migr. Abr.* 9). The passage gives a clue to Philo's standpoint. It is not the body which is inherently bad. But the life of the senses, which finds its material, so to speak, in the physical organisation, is irrational, and nothing but its subordination to the Divine element of reason can preserve the soul from going astray. Accordingly, Philo anticipates St. Paul in using σάρξ, "flesh," to denote the lower side of human nature as realised and felt in an ordinary experience.[1] Only here we come upon an important difference. In *De Gigant.* 40 this noteworthy

---

[1] Lietzmann, *Römerbrief*, p. 37, seems to us completely astray when, in discussing the use of σάρξ by Philo and Paul, he asserts that "in Philo it is viewed entirely from the intellectual standpoint, in Paul from that of pure religion." In our judgment Philo is here far more directly influenced by religious experience than by any philosophical theory.

FUNDAMENTAL PROBLEMS

utterance occurs: "Contrast the good of the flesh with that of the soul (ψυχῆς) and that of the whole. That of the flesh is irrational pleasure, but that of the soul and of the whole is the reason of the universe, even God." Here σάρξ and ψυχή are set in antithesis, a usage never found in Paul. But in the same treatise (§ 29) he says: "The supreme cause of lack of knowledge is the flesh and intimate association with the flesh. Indeed God himself acknowledges this when he affirms that 'because they are flesh' (Gen. vi. 3) the Divine Spirit (πνεῦμα) cannot abide with them." This is a usage extraordinarily akin to Paul's regular contrast between σάρξ and πνεῦμα. It seems highly probable that Philo in using πνεῦμα for the Divine influence or action upon men, a usage foreign to earlier Greek thought, followed the LXX, which regularly translates *ruach*, "spirit" (generally of God), by πνεῦμα. We have little doubt that Paul's employment of it in the same sense also originated there. But Philo differs from Paul in employing σῶμα far more frequently than σάρξ for the irrational part of

FUNDAMENTAL PROBLEMS

human nature, which is liable to temptations to sin through its sense-life; and Philo does not seem to individualise πνεῦμα in Paul's sense of man's higher, rational element (νοῦς) inspired by the Spirit of God.

From what has been said it is, further, clear that Philo uses ψυχή in a sense foreign to Paul. That is to say, for him ψυχή is often equivalent to νοῦς or πνεῦμα, the highest element in human nature, an element which can be distinguished from mere animal life. Examples have been given above. Paul rarely uses ψυχή except in the vague sense of "person" or "personality,"[1] for which *nephesh* constantly stands in the Old Testament, and is generally rendered in this connection by ψυχή in the LXX. Three or four times he employs it, also following a usage of the LXX, in the popular sense of "heart" or "mind," with no emphasis on any psychological *nuance*. Probably the phrase, "your spirit, soul, and body" (1 Thess. v. 23), is more colloquial than anything else, and certainly it is quite unfit to prop up the

[1] About eight instances.

FUNDAMENTAL PROBLEMS

theory of a trichotomy of human nature which has been based upon it. There only remains 1 Cor. xv. 45, where he carefully follows the LXX of Gen. ii. 7, which translates לְנֶפֶשׁ חַיָּה by εἰς ψυχὴν ζῶσαν. Here he deliberately contrasts ψυχή with πνεῦμα, and it becomes clear that in his view ψυχή stands for the life of man as untouched by the Holy Spirit. Of course, this "life" for Paul as for Philo was due to Divine operation, but under the influence of his central conception of the πνεῦμα as God's special gift to the Christian believer, it lay close to Paul's hand to emphasise ψυχή as the "natural" element common to every human being, as contrasted with the "supernatural," which stood supreme. Plainly the adjective ψυχικός, which he uses in 1 Cor. xv., in direct connection with the quotation from the LXX just discussed, and once in 1 Cor. ii., where it also stands in sharp antithesis to πνευματικός, has its meaning determined by this contrast with πνεῦμα. In this case, again, we note the divergence in Philo. He employs ψυχικός repeatedly, in all sorts of connections. In a

FUNDAMENTAL PROBLEMS

few instances it applies to the ordinary *inner life* of men, whether viewed as physical, or as the sphere of feeling and other forms of consciousness.[1] More often it occurs in the higher sense of "spiritual," which is, of course, totally alien to Paul.[2] But it is easy to see how readily his use of the term might glide into that of Paul if he had occasion to employ it in contrasting the irrational with the rational part of the soul.

In Philo, νοῦς is often interchangeable with ψυχή, although, of course, it usually stands for the higher aspect of the soul. Here Paul approximates to his older contemporary. For he regards νοῦς as an important element in the natural equipment of man, his highest capacity apart from the Divine gift of the πνεῦμα.

---

[1] E.g. (*a*) *De Op. M.* 66 : σωματικῆς ἢ ψυχικῆς οὐσίας ; (*b*) *Leg. Alleg.* ii. 85 : τὸν ψυχικὸν ὄχλον σκεδάσαντος θεοῦ, of the tumult of the sense-life, but with no necessary suggestion of evil ; (*c*) *ibid.* ii. 22, where the powers of the νοῦς are described as ἑκτικήν, φυτικήν, ψυχικήν, λογικήν, διανοητικήν.

[2] E.g. *Leg. Alleg.* i. 97 : τροφῆς ψυχικῆς ; *ibid.* iii. 171 : φωτὸς κοινωνῆσαι ψυχικοῦ ; *ibid.* 145 : τῶν ψυχικῶν ἀγαθῶν ; *Quod det. pot.* : τὸν ψυχικὸν θάνατον ; *De Spec. Leg.* iv. 75 : κληρονόμους τοῦ ψυχικοῦ πλούτου. With this use agrees the only example in the LXX, 4 Macc. i. 32, where desires are divided into higher, ψυχικαί, and lower, σωματικαί.

FUNDAMENTAL PROBLEMS

Thus in Rom. vii. 25 he contrasts νοῦς with σάρξ, an antithesis in which from his standpoint ψυχή could not have replaced it. On the other hand, except in a quotation from Isa. xl. 13 (LXX), he clearly distinguishes νοῦς from πνεῦμα. For while νοῦς is the most spiritual element in the "natural" man, it has to be renewed (Rom. xii. 2). It still belongs to the life of the σάρξ (Col. ii. 18). When renewed, it exercises a most important function. It becomes the rational faculty in the new life of the Spirit, and as such regulates the exuberant enthusiasm of the pneumatic life (1 Cor. xiv. 14 f., 19). As passages which we have quoted show, Philo uses πνεῦμα in a much larger range of meanings than Paul. In the former it is sometimes equivalent to reason, e.g. *Quod det. pot.* 84, where he describes it as the energy of the ψυχή, "that Godlike product by which we reason." It also represents the activity of the senses (e.g. *De Fuga*, 182), where it is associated with sight, hearing, smell, etc. Finally, it denotes the Divine Spirit in a unique sense, manifested in men of notable wisdom (e.g.

FUNDAMENTAL PROBLEMS

De Gig. 23) or prophetic power (e.g. *Quis Rer. Div. H.* 255). This last usage, directly based on the Old Testament, is closely akin to that of Paul in the Christian sphere, which is mainly the result of personal religious experience, and so πνεῦμα becomes the *terminus technicus* for the Divine life in the believer.

CHAPTER IV

MAN'S YEARNING FOR GOD

THE earnest longing of men for God is recognised by Philo from various standpoints. Sometimes it is viewed under a more abstract aspect, rather as the satisfaction of the intellect than of the whole nature. "There is nothing better," he says, "than to search after the true God, even if the finding of him should escape human capacity, seeing that even eagerness of desire to understand him in itself produces unspeakable pleasures and delights" (*De Spec. Leg.* i. 36). Similarly, in *De Confus. Ling.* 97: "It befits those who would company with knowledge to strive after a vision of the Existent, and if they cannot attain this, at least of his image, the most sacred Logos, and next in order of that most perfect of his works, this universe of ours." But in other

MAN'S YEARNING FOR GOD

passages we find a far more personal note. "To what soul," he asks, "was it given to put evil out of sight, save to that to which God was revealed, the soul which he deemed worthy of his unspeakable mysteries? For he says, Shall I hide from Abraham, my servant, the things I do? True, O Saviour, for thine own works thou dost show to the soul that yearns for goodness, and hidest none of them from her. For this reason she is able to flee from evil . . . and unceasingly to extirpate hurtful passions" (*Leg. Alleg.* iii. 27). Again, commenting on God's word (Gen. xlvi. 4), "I will go down with thee," he expands as follows: "This I do because of my pity for thy rational nature, so that by my guidance thou mayest be brought up out of the Hades of passion to the Olympian abode of virtue, for to all suppliant souls I have made known the way that leads to heaven, preparing for them a thoroughfare that they might not grow weary of their journey" (*De Post. Cain.* 31). Let us inquire what he means by "the Hades of passion," and how souls are to flee from evil.

MAN'S YEARNING FOR GOD

(a) *The Meaning of Sin*

Philo's conception of sin is indissolubly associated with his view of men's bodily nature which we have just examined. Here, as in the case of all his positions, we must not be influenced by isolated passages, but by the trend of his thought as a whole. Thus, a statement like *Leg. Alleg.* iii. 71: "The body is evil by nature and plots against the soul," is a bare summary which in no way exhibits the processes of Philo's reflection. Nor do we get upon the right track either by pointing decisively to his theory of the descent of souls into human bodies or by emphasising the frequent descriptions of the Fall of man in Paradise. The former, as already noted, appears to us a side-issue for Philo. In the latter he probably uses the figure of Adam as a sort of inclusive personification of humanity, much as Paul did in Rom. v. 12 ff. Philo really starts from his experience of human nature in himself and from his observation of his fellow-men, the precise standpoint of Paul in all that he

MAN'S YEARNING FOR GOD

affirms regarding "the flesh." Of course Philo, from the texture of his mind, is compelled to theorise on the subject. But that is subsequent to his acquaintance with the conflicts of the moral life. The personal note, so poignant in some of his utterances, gives the real key to his starting-point: e.g. *Leg. Alleg.* iii. 211: "There is another kind of groaning found in those who repent and are distressed because of their past waywardness, who exclaim, Wretched men that we are, who have for so long been stricken, without knowing it, by the disease of senselessness, folly and wrong pursuits." We naturally compare Paul's famous ejaculation (Rom. vii. 24): "Wretched man that I am, who shall deliver me from the body of this death?"

Bearing in mind, then, the point from which he starts, we must further note that there are certain presuppositions about which he never argues. The body is, as we have seen, for Philo as for Paul, a clog upon the higher nature. He would have identified himself whole-heartedly with the Apostle's self-revelation: "I beat my body black and

MAN'S YEARNING FOR GOD

blue and make it my slave" (1 Cor. ix. 27). This is not because its material is evil, but because it is indissolubly bound up with the life of sense. That life is largely at the mercy of pleasure (ἡδονή), an irrational and seductive passion. Pleasure is the serpent, "an abominable thing in itself" (*Leg. Alleg.* iii. 68), which "beguiles and leads astray the reason" (*ibid.* 64). The "love of pleasure" is "ungodly" (*ibid.* iii. 211). So that when Philo speaks of sinning as "innate in every man who has come into being" (*De Vita Mos.* ii. (iii.) 147), when he describes as "without limit" "the things that stain the soul" (*De Mut. Nom.* 49), he has above all else in view the appeal of passion to man's nature. "Passion," he declares, "is the fountain of sins" (*Quod Deus sit immut.* 72). But there is nothing mechanical in the working of this appeal. The allurements of passion present themselves before the will. Philo assumes man's power of choice. "Moses," he observes, "does not follow the opinion of some impious men who say that God is the cause of evils, but

MAN'S YEARNING FOR GOD

he attributes them to our own hands, meaning by that our own efforts and the voluntary turning of the mind toward the worse" (*Quod det. pot.* 122). Involuntary sin occupies a position between right and wrong (*Quaestt. in Gen.* iv. § 64). Philo describes his view of such sin with perfect clearness. "As long," he says, "as we only form unworthy conceptions by mere imagination, we are not responsible for our thoughts, for the soul can have a direction given to it involuntarily. But when action follows deliberation that deliberation may be put to our account, for in this way especially voluntary error is revealed" (*Quod det. pot.* 97). Accordingly he can allege that "mind and reason are, as it were, the home of vice and virtue, in which it is their nature to dwell" (*De Op. M.* 73). Man deliberately subordinates the higher rational life of the soul to the sway of irrational desire, instead of following the counsel of Moses that we "ought to cut out and root up passion from the soul" (*Leg. Alleg.* iii. 129).

What is the bearing of this upon God? It is true, as Windisch (*Die Frömmigkeit*

MAN'S YEARNING FOR GOD

Philos, p. 98) observes, that in Philo guilt before God is overshadowed by the sense of man's nothingness as a creature in the Divine presence. Yet there are hints of something more positive. "God was justly angry at them," he says, speaking of the generation described in Gen. vi., "seeing that the living creature which seemed to be the noblest and had been judged worthy of kinship with himself, because of sharing with him in reason, eagerly followed evil and every kind of evil, when it ought to have practised goodness" (*De Abr.* 41). Man, that is to say, knew the ideal and deliberately ignored it. God entrusted to him the gifts of soul, speech and the sense-life. But by far the majority of of men, under the influence of self-love (φιλαυτία), appropriated these for themselves. They had their just reward in souls defiled by irrational passions and held in the grasp of innumerable vices: in speech whetted against the truth, hurtful to those who heard it, disgraceful to those who uttered it: in a sense-life insatiable, heedless of all controlling influence (*Quis Rer. Div. H.* 106 ff.).

MAN'S YEARNING FOR GOD

This self-love, which prompts to the abuse of men's God-given powers, reveals itself flagrantly in the form of τῦφος, overweening vanity, which is again and again emphasised by Philo. He asserts that "τῦφος is the artificer of many other evils, of false pretension, of arrogance, of inequality.... By reason of τῦφος even Divine things are utterly scorned" (*De Decal.* 5 ff.). This entire attitude means defiance of God, and it may become so hardened that doom is inevitable. Commenting on the subject of vows and pledges by which maidens, wives, widows, or divorced wives bind their souls, as discussed in Num. xxx., he makes a psychological application of the law's prescriptions. The understanding can bind itself down to courses which are for ever incurable. It will thus not only be widowed of knowledge but divorced from it. "That is to say: the soul which is bereft of good, but not yet divorced from it, can by steadfastness find terms of reconciliation with right reason, her lawful husband; but that which has been once divorced and made to live apart as un-

MAN'S YEARNING FOR GOD

faithful has lost her chance for ever and can no more return to her old home" (*Quod det. pot.* 148 f. Cf. the stern utterance of *Qu. in Gen.* i. 70). Yet, though the only fitting punishment for the human race was "that it should be extirpated on account of its ingratitude towards God, its benefactor and Saviour, God in his mercy took pity upon men, and moderated their penalty" (*De Op. M.* 169). Necessarily, however, the Divine grace presupposes minds and hearts which through repentance and humility can respond to its workings.

In theory, Philo may at times be disposed to associate wrong action with man's constitution as a transient being, just as there are passages in St. Paul which appear, on the surface, to connect sin with man's physical heritage. But in reality, for both, sin means an assent of the will to the lower, selfish impulses, in opposition to those which point God-wards. The actual human experience which they both know presents the spectacle of a practical rather than a theoretical dualism. Wrong-doing in the strict sense is not in-

MAN'S YEARNING FOR GOD

voluntary, the result of ignorance. It is the turning away from God in favour of self, which Philo calls τροπή. The situation is that of a being akin to God, participating in the Divine Logos or Thought, and yet exposed to the assaults of pleasurable cravings, with which his reason identifies itself and makes them the ends of living. Men's inner life, that is to say, is, "mingled of opposing qualities, right and wrong, base and honourable, good and evil" (*Qu. in. Gen.* iv. 203). Philo quotes with approval the saying of Epicharmus : "Whosoever yields but slightly to evil is a very good man : for no one is guiltless, no one is exempt from reproach." Hence the main task, if any spiritual progress is to be made, must be the attainment of self-knowledge. "Hither, you who are stuffed full of vanity and indiscipline and braggart boasting, you pretenders to wisdom, who claim not only to know clearly everything that is, but also, in your hardihood, venture to declare their causes, as if you had been present at the creation of the world. . . . Once for all, let alone these other concerns :

MAN'S YEARNING FOR GOD

know yourselves, and declare plainly of what nature you are" (*De Migr. Abr.* 136 f.).

(*b*) *Conscience*

At this point in his reflection Philo enunciates with spiritual insight and power a truth of the inner life which up till now had been but dimly foreshadowed, viz. the existence of the moral consciousness, a criterion of action placed at men's disposal, with boundless possibilities for the building up of human character in accordance with the Divine purpose. He has, indeed, no formal discussion of Conscience and its functions, but his frequent references to its commanding position within the soul reveal its importance for his thought. Here, as invariably, his utterances are found to fluctuate, but their general drift is easy to grasp.

There are several important passages in which his view of Conscience closely approaches Paul's conception of νοῦς, the higher element in human nature which approves of the good (*e.g.* Rom. vii. 23, 25). This Paul occasionally designates ὁ ἔσω ἄνθρωπος, "the

MAN'S YEARNING FOR GOD

man within." It assents to the Divine order (Rom. vii. 22); it is renewed in the Christian (2 Cor. iv. 16); it is the recipient of the power of the Spirit (Eph. iii. 16). In other words, it is the connecting link between the "natural" and the "supernatural." Now, in *De Agricult.* 9, Philo asks: "What can be the man in each of us but the νοῦς which is wont to reap the benefits of those things which have been sown and planted?" A further stage in the working out of the idea appears in *De Fuga*, 131: "These are the utterances of the genuine man, who is (reading with Cohn, ὅς ἐστι) the testing power (ἔλεγχος) of the soul, who, when he sees the soul in perplexity making inquiry and search, takes care that she may not go astray and miss the right path." It should be noted that ἔλεγχος is for Philo an almost technical description of the function of Conscience. The full-fledged conception is found in *Quod det. pot.* 22 f.: "If the vision of their soul had not been defective, they would have recognised that the precise and characteristic name of the genuine man is just 'man'

MAN'S YEARNING FOR GOD

(ἄνθρωπος), the proper designation of the well-knit and rational understanding (διανοίας). This man who dwells in the soul of each is found to be, on the one hand, ruler and king, on the other, judge and umpire in the contests of life, and at times taking the place of witness or accuser he tests us invisibly within, not allowing us to open our mouth, but laying hold of and bridling with the reins of conscience the stubborn and rebellious course of the tongue, and thus brings it to a halt." Here Philo assigns to the rational understanding the function of moral judgment, regarding it no doubt in its unsullied character as the commanding element in the inner world of the soul. Hence it is not a mere accommodation to popular usage, as Bréhier supposes (*op. cit.* p. 302), when, in *De Decal.* 87, Philo describes as *innate* (συμπεφυκώς) to every soul the "testing power" (ὁ ἔλεγχος) that dwells with us, that is always true to its character of hating evil and loving good, that, as accuser, blames, accuses, frowns upon us, and again as judge, teaches, warns, exhorts us to change our

MAN'S YEARNING FOR GOD

ways. That is surely one permanent aspect of the situation. It entirely accords with the well-known statement of *De Op. M.* 146 : " Every man, so far as his understanding (διάνοια) is concerned, is intimately related to the Divine Logos, an impress or particle or effulgence of the blessed nature, while as regards his bodily status he is closely akin to the whole cosmos." This is what Paul means when he speaks of man as the "image" and "reflection" of God (1 Cor. xi. 7). Were this not true, man would be in the position of the irrational creatures, having no spiritual affinity to the Divine, and finally excluded from fellowship with God.

But Philo, like Paul, recognises the irrational tendency in human nature to follow the worse, although it knows the better. Therefore man's mind has to be reinforced in its moral aspirations by the Divine energy itself. And so, repeatedly, Philo identifies Conscience with the Logos. Perhaps the most notable passage is *Quod Deus sit immut.* 134 ff. : " So long as the Divine Logos has not come into our soul as into its abode, the deeds of the soul are blameless: for its guardian or father or teacher or whatever we ought to call that Priest by whom alone it can be warned and controlled remains far away from it: and those who sin through ignorance, without knowledge of what things they ought to do, receive pardon. For they do not even apprehend their actions as sins. Indeed they even suppose that they are acting rightly in cases where they commit great errors. But when the Priest who genuinely tests us enters into us like a perfectly pure ray of light, then we recognise the unrighteous designs harboured in our soul and our culpable ... deeds. All these the consecrated testing Power, having shown their defilement, bids us pack away and strip off, that he may behold the house of the soul clean, and if any diseases have arisen in it, may heal them." And later, in the same context, having compared the Logos to a prophet, on the basis of 1 Kings xvii. 18, he continues: "For this inspired being, in the grasp of an Olympian love, and goaded by the irresistible stings of his Divine frenzy, entering into the soul, creates there the remembrance of her old wrong-doings and sins, not that she may again yield to them, but that with loud lamentations and weeping she may come back from her former wandering, hating its issue, and may follow the promptings of the Logos-prophet, who is the interpreter of God."

Here the clearest emphasis is laid upon Conscience as the Divine agent in the soul, so illuminating its actions that their real character cannot escape detection. Philo never inquires whether this is a gradual process, accompanying or constituting the moral growth of the individual, or a sudden experience, which might be compared to Paul's remarkable account (Rom. vii. 7 ff.) of his awakening to the real meaning of sin. The opening sentences of the passage inevitably remind us, up to a certain point, of what the Apostle says about sin not being reckoned to a man so long as no moral standard like the law confronts him. But for Philo the activity of conscience is wholly and permanently salutary, while by Paul the

MAN'S YEARNING FOR GOD

religion of law comes to be regarded merely as a makeshift.

Bréhier (*op. cit.* p. 301) observes that the function ascribed by the Stoics to the Wise Man as a consultant on the subject of moral health and progress is by Philo entrusted to Conscience. This marks a real epoch in the history of ethics. The Greek schools had been chiefly concerned with the question of the highest good for man. When, in their later phases, they came to discuss the source of moral obligation, the Stoics, who led the way, found the authoritative norm in reason. That doctrine is, as we have seen, recognised by Philo, but in a very real sense he transforms it on lines akin to, although not immediately derived from, Old Testament religion. For we may at least say that Jeremiah's great conception of the Divine law or teaching written in men's hearts approximates to Philo's position. Essentially, for Philo, Conscience involves the impact of God upon the soul. It is the assessor in the nature of the inner life (*De Jos.* 47 f.). It is an angel who, while it questions the soul in

MAN'S YEARNING FOR GOD

order to reveal to it the truth, has full knowledge of the situation (*De Fuga*, 203 f.). It is identified with the vision of the good which often hovers suddenly over the most worthless, but which they are unable to grasp or to retain. And this vision is nothing else than a visitation of the Spirit of God (*De Gig.* 210 f.). This last passage brings out clearly what is suggested by Philo's entire conception of conscience, its remarkable affinity to the idea of the "advocate" (παράκλητος) in such places as John xvi. 8 : " When he has come, he will convict (ἐλέγξει) the world as regards sin and righteousness and judgment" : and xix. 17 : " He will give you another advocate to be with you for ever, the spirit of truth." There is a remarkable passage in Philo which gives an almost startling corroboration of this. When dealing (*De Spec. Leg.* i. 235 ff.) with legal enactments bearing on the case of those who have defrauded their neighbour and afterwards confessed their sin, he says: " After making atonement to the person he has wronged, Moses enjoins that he should go to the holy place, to ask for remission of his sins, bringing with him an irreproachable advocate (παράκλητος), the power which has searched his soul,[1] which delivered him from a hopeless calamity, ridding him of a mortal disease and transforming him into a condition of perfect health."

We have seen that the main function of Conscience in Philo is ἔλεγχος, testing or convicting. And for him its witness is incorruptible and absolutely true (*De Post. Cain.* 59). Its activity at least points in the direction of Paul's great doctrine of the Spirit as the Divine life in the Christian, although, of course, that presupposes a background of experience which Philo would scarcely have understood. Indeed, Philo seems to identify Conscience with God himself. " If the understanding, supposing that it can do wrong without the knowledge of the Deity, as if he were not able to see everything, commits sin stealthily and in secret places, and afterwards, whether of itself or at the suggestion of some one, perceives that it is impossible for anything to be concealed from

[1] τὸν κατὰ ψυχὴν ἔλεγχον.

MAN'S YEARNING FOR GOD

God, and thus unfolds itself and all its habits, and bringing them forth as to the sunlight shows them to the Overseer of all things, asserting its penitence for these wrong opinions which formerly it cherished through lack of knowledge . . . it is purified and benefited and assuages the just wrath of that testing, punitive Power which stands over it" (*De Somn.* i. 91).

Reviewing, then, all the evidence we have examined, it may be truly affirmed that Philo regards Conscience as a real factor in awakening man's aspirations after God. An indispensable condition, therefore, of reaching God is the lowliness of the man who is able justly to estimate himself as in the Divine presence. "I have learnt to measure my own nothingness and to admire the exceeding excellence of thy benefits. And when I perceive myself to be but 'dust and ashes' and whatever can be more despicable, then I have the courage to meet thee, having become humble, cast down to the ground" (*Quis Rer. Div. H.* 29).

MAN'S YEARNING FOR GOD

(c) *Repentance*

If Conscience stimulates the soul to moral progress, the fundamental step in such progress is Repentance. Philo definitely associates this change of mental and moral direction with the action of conscience. When discussing, on the basis of Lev. vi. 2 ff., the case of a man who has sworn falsely regarding a wrong he has done his neighbour, he remarks that the man, having imagined that he has escaped the charge brought against him, "becomes his own accuser, being convicted inwardly by conscience, and reproaches himself for his falsehood, and making open confession of his wrong-doing, asks pardon." In such a case he is bidden to prove the genuineness of his repentance, not by words but by deeds. And Philo points out that the sin-offering he has to present is the same in kind as the peace-offering (τοῦ σωτηρίου θυσία), "for in a sense the man who repents is saved, turning aside from that disease of the soul which is more serious than bodily passions" (*De Spec. Leg.*

MAN'S YEARNING FOR GOD

i. 235 ff.). This instance shows his view of the direct effect of conscience upon the will in the matter of repentance. Probably that remains a presupposition. But his delicate moral observation plays on the subject from varying standpoints, which suggests that he is influenced not by theory but by practical experience.

The main root of Repentance is the discovery of the soul that it has been turning aside from God after lower aims, such as pleasure. At this discovery, "the man, beholding God, laments over his own desertion . . . and his soul cries out, imploring the Almighty to save him from further deviation and to accomplish his perfecting" (*Leg. All.* iii. 211 ff.). Repentance therefore begins in grief of spirit. "Those who genuinely repent are afflicted by reason of their former course of life, and in their grief at its wretchedness they weep, they groan, they sigh" (*Qu. in Exod.* i. 15). Sometimes the emphasis is laid on the causality of the Divine Mercy, which is no doubt assumed by Philo in all the operations of conscience. "He resolved

on confession and pardon at an earlier time:
now . . . he appoints repentance, not scoffing
at nor reproaching in any way those who are
thought to have sinned, making possible the
ascent of the soul from vice to goodness"
(*Qu. in Gen.* i. 82). Whatever be the
immediate stimulus, a primary stage in the
process of repenting consists in confession of
sins. "If . . . in shame they turn with
their whole soul, reproaching themselves for
their waywardness, declaring and confessing
all their sins, in the first place with purified
mind before conscience . . . and then with
their lips . . . they shall obtain the favour
of the gracious God, the Saviour, who has
imparted to the race of men his choice and
chiefest gift, intimate kinship with his own
Logos" (*De Exsecr.* 163). But besides the
negative element of penitence, repentance
involves the positive longing for goodness.
"Following upon the victory gained by hope,
there is a second contest in which the repenting soul is the competitor, for though it has
not participated in the unchanging nature
. . . which always remains the same, yet

MAN'S YEARNING FOR GOD

suddenly possessed by a passion . . . for the nobler, it hastens to abandon its habitual greed and wrong-doing, and to make its abode with self-control and righteousness and the other virtues" (*De Praem. et Poen.* 15).

In the passage just quoted Repentance is made to follow Hope. This is a favourite position of Philo's. Hope he regards as the supreme characteristic of the human soul (*De Abr.* 8), in the sense of the expectation of good things. Its precise relation to repentance is described in a passage where Philo groups them both with complete attainment (τελειότης). But to understand the significance of this, we must turn to an earlier statement. "It must be noted," he says, "that repentance is ranked second to complete attainment, as a change from sickness to health ranks second to a perfectly sound body. Thus uninterrupted completeness in virtue stands closest to Divine power, while the improvement that has gone on for some time is the special blessing of a well-ordered soul, refusing to continue among childish things, but with full-grown and

MAN'S YEARNING FOR GOD

manly bent, seeking a condition of poise, and following the vision of the good" (*De Abr.* 26). In the light of these words we can appreciate the later utterance: "The perfect man is complete from the beginning: he who has repented is half-made, having devoted the former period of his life to evil, and the later to virtue, to which he . . . transformed his abode; while he that hopes . . . is defective, aiming always at the good, but having not yet been able to reach it, resembling sailors who, though eager to put into port, are still at sea, unable to get to anchorage" (*ibid.* 47). Probably, as in the case of the Wise Man of the Stoics, the position of the τέλειος is for Philo an ideal rather than an attainment. For, in another important passage where again he assigns to Repentance the second rank, he remarks: "To commit no sin at all is peculiar to God, possibly also to a Divine man, but to turn from sin to a blameless life is the part of a discerning man who recognises what is wholly profitable" (*De Virtut.* 177). In drawing an ingenious distinction between the first

MAN'S YEARNING FOR GOD

and the second return of the dove to Noah, he uses the legend to emphasise the *gradual* process of repentance. "To find repentance is not easy, but an excessively difficult and toilsome business": and he proceeds to illustrate the stages in the process by the olive-leaf and the dry twig (LXX of Gen. viii. 11) in the dove's mouth (*Qu. in Gen.* ii. 42 f.). We do not touch on an interesting feature of his longest discussion of repentance (*De Virtut.* 175 ff.), in which he deals primarily with the turning of idol-worshippers to the one God, and shows that this involves the exchange of folly for insight and of wrongdoing for righteousness. The final result of Repentance, which unifies the life of the soul, is that its subject becomes at one and the same time beloved of God and a lover of Him.

(*d*) Faith

If we were attempting to discuss the genetic development of the Christian soul on New Testament lines, it would be natural, after estimating the significance of Repentance, to deal with the fundamental religious

MAN'S YEARNING FOR GOD

relationship of Faith. In a sense this is also legitimate for the student of Philo. But that sense must be made clear. Repentance, as we have seen, means that conscience has been at work, unveiling to the soul its own unworthiness, and urging it on to a nobler course. Faith, in Philo, seems to presuppose this background. Whatever else it may be, it is at least "an amelioration of the soul at all points," but "of the soul resting and established on the Cause of all things, who is able for anything, but who wills the best" (*De Abr.* 268). The latter part of this description embodies much of Philo's doctrine of Faith.

It is important to notice that he is largely guided in his conception by the Old Testament report of Abraham's faith, and especially by Gen. xv. 6: "Abraham believed (ἐπίστευσε) God, and it was counted to him for righteousness," a passage which is equally prominent in Paul, and seems to have taken an outstanding place in Synagogue theology (see, e.g., *Mechilta*, ed. Winter u. Wünsche, p. 110). That fact, which has numerous

MAN'S YEARNING FOR GOD

parallels throughout his works, reminds us that some of his observations on Faith are not necessarily typical of his thought, but due rather to the details which happen to make up some passage in the story of Abraham.[1] But in the main his own view accords with the Old Testament account of the patriarch's faith. And his description of it is most significant for his entire outlook. " He first is said to have believed God, since he was the first to possess an unwavering and stable notion (ὑπόληψιν) that the sole Cause is the highest, and that his providence is over the universe and all that belongs to it. So having come to possess faith, the most stable of the virtues, he entered into possession of all the others along with it" (*De Virtut.* 216). This, although expressed in different terminology, is in remarkable agreement with Paul's interpretation of the same story, that

---

[1] This consideration takes from the force of Dr. Bigg's remark (*Christian Platonists of Alexandria*, p. 26) that in *Quis Rer. Div. H.* § 21, Philo associates Faith with a lower stage of spiritual life. Philo is attempting to do full justice to all the details of the special passage he is expounding (Gen. xv. 8).

MAN'S YEARNING FOR GOD

Abraham staked everything on his conviction of the grace and truth and power of God (Rom. iv. 16 ff. ; Gal. iii. 7 ff., 18). In both cases there is far more than the mere unfaltering expectation of good things to come. The very foundation of religion is implied in this relation of absolute trust in the unseen God. The same may be said of the writer to the Hebrews, who stands in line with Philo at so many points. For him faith is "the assurance of the things hoped for, the proof (or, conviction, ἔλεγχος) of the things not seen" (xi. 1). It means the realisation in this present of that invisible realm in which God can be fully known, or rather, the realisation of the unseen God himself. "For Moses . . . endured as seeing him who is invisible" (xi. 27). The assurance of God is primary for the writer to the Hebrews as for Philo. All fulfilment of hopes and expectations is for both bound up with that. Indeed, the New Testament teacher uses language which might have been Philo's own, when he declares : "He that draws near to God must believe that he exists, and that he

MAN'S YEARNING FOR GOD

rewards those who earnestly seek him" (xi. 6). This conviction transforms life from illusion into reality.

In emphasising the profoundly religious significance of faith in Philo, as contrasted with a more superficial aspect of it, namely, belief in the fulfilment of God's promises before there is any sign of its approach, Bréhier (*op. cit.* p. 222 f.) suggests that the deeper view is due to the influence of Stoic mysticism.[1] And he attempts to find a confirmation of this in such statements as *Quis Rer. Div. H.* 101 : "That it would come to pass, he of course firmly grasped in accordance with the Divine promises," where he associates the "firm grasp" with the Stoic idea of faith as "powerful apprehension." It is possible that some of his terms may have been suggested by Stoic usage, although they are such as might naturally present themselves. But Bréhier's own admission (*loc. cit.*) that, in distinction from the Stoics, who use the conception in reference to all true representations, Philo never applies the idea of

[1] So also W. H. P. Hatch, *The Pauline Idea of Faith*, p. 47.

MAN'S YEARNING FOR GOD

faith except to God, makes it far more probable that he speaks fundamentally on the ground of his own religious experience.

When we try to analyse Philo's view of Faith more clearly, we are at once impressed by its intellectual side. That has come out above in the important passage where he describes it as a stable ὑπόληψις, and is corroborated by the quotations from Hebrews which have so markedly Philonic a colour. "To clear away each of these [earthly influences] and to distrust the world of becoming which is of itself wholly unworthy of confidence, and to have faith in God alone, who alone is in truth trustworthy, requires a large and Olympian understanding, one which is no longer enticed by our worldly interests" (*Quis Rer. Div. H.* 93). Hence Schlatter is so far justified in saying that for Philo, Faith is "the fruit of knowledge, and the incompleteness of the latter is directly transferred to it" (*Der Glaube im NT.* p. 92). But obviously all Faith involves intellectual elements. The question is whether it gets beyond this intellectual

MAN'S YEARNING FOR GOD

starting-point. And it is not difficult to answer that question in Philo's case.

In one of his numerous comments on Gen. xv. 6 he asks: "In what else can we put our faith [save in God]? Can we put it in leadership or reputations and distinctions, or in abundance of riches and high birth, or in health and quick sensibility, or in vigour and bodily beauty?" After estimating these at their proper worth, which at best is utterly transient, he concludes: "Faith towards God alone is a true and stable good, a consolation of life, a fulfilment of bright hopes, a famine of evils, and a full crop of blessings. . . . For, as those who walk by a slippery path stumble and fall, while they who tread the dry high road go forward without tripping, so those who engross their soul with bodily and external interests accustom it to nothing but falls . . . while they who through the contemplation of virtue hasten towards God, follow a straight course. . . . So that one may truly say that he who has put his faith in the former objects refuses to trust God, while he who refuses to

MAN'S YEARNING FOR GOD

trust them has put his faith in God" (*De Abr.* 263, 268 f.). It is plain that by genuine Faith, Philo means that liberation of the soul from the dominion of earthly good which has as its obverse side the great venture of casting one's self upon God. This he describes as a straining, testing experience. Referring to Gen. xv. 6 as a eulogy of the trusting soul, he meets a possible objection : " Perhaps some one might say, Do you judge this worthy of praise ? Who would refuse to heed the word and promise of God, even if he were the most lawless and impious of men ? Our reply would be : Dear friend, do not without careful inquiry deprive the wise man of the eulogy which is his due, or ascribe to the worthless the most perfect of virtues, faith, or find fault with our discernment in such matters. For if you choose to make a profounder search and not merely a superficial one, you will clearly discover that it is not easy to put faith in God alone without dragging in something else, on account of the close kinship which binds us to mortal things, a kinship which persuades us to confide in

MAN'S YEARNING FOR GOD

money and fame, and power and friends and vigour of body and many similar things. . . . To fix our moorings firmly . . . in the Existent alone is a surprising thing among men, who do not possess unadulterated good, but not strange when truth is in control, rather the pure product of righteousness" (*Quis Rer. Div. H.* 90 ff.). Here he deliberately excludes everything but the immediate relation of the soul to God. God fills the entire spiritual horizon: and there is no other. This is the true paradox of religious experience: to distrust and detach one's self from all the forces that press in upon human life, as deceptive and unreal, and to hazard everything upon the Invisible, which cannot be apprehended by the ordinary process of knowledge. This implies a tremendous act and perseverance of will. Philo is true to his Old Testament lineage. There is nothing to correspond to it in his Greek masters. Knowledge could not achieve such a result. And the issue is a glad fearlessness of bearing (παρρησία). Philo delights to dwell upon this. "The noble man"—he is describing

MAN'S YEARNING FOR GOD

Moses and his attitude towards God—"can behave with such glad fearlessness as not merely to speak and shout, but he will actually dare as the result of pure trust and genuine feeling to cry out" (*Quis Rer. Div. H.* 19). But such an attitude, the high product of faith, is devoid of presumption. It never crosses the boundary which separates confidence in God from self-confidence. "What am I"—Philo represents Abraham as saying—"that thou shouldest impart to me of thy speech? Am not I an exile from my country?... Am not I an alien from my father's house?... But thou, O Lord, art to me my country, thou art my kinsfolk, ... thou art my reward, my glad fearlessness.... Why then should not I dare to utter my thoughts?... Yet I who speak of daring confess my awe and terror.... Without ceasing, therefore, I find delight in this blending, which has moved me neither to speak boldly without godly fear, nor to tremble before God without glad fearlessness" (*ibid.* 26 ff.). Philo's descriptions of παρρησία at once recall the prominence of the idea in

MAN'S YEARNING FOR GOD

Hebrews and *1 John*. In the former it belongs distinctly, as in Philo, to the sphere of faith. Indeed, chap. iii. 6 might have come from the older author: "whose house are we, if we keep our glad fearlessness and our exultant hope stable unto the end." But not less remarkable is the Johannine usage. True, it is based on love rather than faith, but it would be hard to distinguish in 1 John between the two. At any rate, for the writer, love is that which unites with God, the very function which faith discharges, according to Philo.

This reference to the New Testament suggests a further one, which will serve to bring out an additional element in Philo's conception of Faith. We have mentioned points in which St. Paul and Philo coincide. And our last paragraph emphasises another, faith's office of linking the soul to God. From the nature of the case, Paul's conception is far more concrete and personal, for its medium is the living person of the living Lord. But besides, for Paul, faith marks especially the initiation of the Chris-

MAN'S YEARNING FOR GOD

tian career. Undoubtedly he presupposes faith at every stage, as so crucial a passage as Gal. ii. 20 demonstrates. But above all, in Paul's view, faith is that movement of the whole being which, in response to the revelation of the Divine love in Jesus Christ, crucified and risen, carries it into union with the living Lord, so that henceforth it shares His attitude to sin and to God.

Some of the passages already cited hint that at times Faith is viewed by Philo not so much in relation to the beginning of a higher life as to its consummation: not so much as a starting-point, but rather as a goal. Commenting on the expression, "which I *will* show you" (Gen. xii. 1), he observes that here God "has carefully defined beforehand for his promise, not the present but the future, as a testimony to the faith which the soul placed in God, not showing forth its gratitude as the result of something accomplished for it, but as springing from its expectation of what was to come. In depending on and clinging to a bright hope, and regarding as indubitably present that

MAN'S YEARNING FOR GOD

which was not present, on account of the steadfastness of him who had made the promise, it has *won as its prize*, faith, a perfect good" (*De Migr. Abr.* 43 f.) This accords with his statement, quoted above, as to the difficulty of attaining to faith. But Philo's attitude is most clearly disclosed in several estimates of Abraham, the typical believer. "He who was the first to forsake empty pride for truth, who used for his perfecting the virtue which could teach[1] him, wins faith towards God as his prize. . . . He to whom it has been granted to despise and overstep all that is corporeal and all that is not, and to rest and establish himself on God alone with steadfast reason and unwavering . . . faith, he is truly fortunate and thrice-blessed. We must also inquire into the fact that each of the three [patriarchs] had assigned to him the prize most befitting. For to him who was perfected by instruction [Abraham] faith was awarded, since the learner must believe his teacher in the lessons he has given: for it is difficult,

[1] Reading διδασκαλικῇ, with Mangey.

MAN'S YEARNING FOR GOD

nay, impossible, to train one who refuses to trust you" (*De Praem. et Poen.* 27, 30, 49). In these passages, emphasis is certainly laid upon faith as the climax of a period of spiritual discipline. But perhaps faith must always be viewed under these two aspects: as the clue to spiritual progress as well as its crown. That is implied in the famous words of Heb. xii. 1 f.: "Let us by endurance run the race that is set before us, looking away to Jesus, the leader and the perfecter of our faith." And no less so in Paul's ardent aspiration (Phil. iii. 8 f.): "Nay, I count all things as loss compared to the surpassing worth of knowing Christ Jesus my Lord . . . that I may win Christ, and be found at the end in him." Faith, and still more faith, is the goal of Paul's striving to the close. It is the supreme issue for all believers.

(*e*) *Immortality*

For Philo, the soul which is linked to God by a real faith must possess eternal life. From various passages it might be inferred that Philo presupposed the immortality of

MAN'S YEARNING FOR GOD

the soul. And this is possibly a necessary corollary of his view of its nature, even though we come upon such a passage as *De Abr.* 55: "The nature of man is mortal." This, in all likelihood, refers to his nature as compound, although perhaps our author has fundamentally in view rather the immortality of the soul than that of human beings as such. But it was not a mere abstract conception which interested Philo. It was the craving for life. His attitude towards this perfection of being continually reminds us of the New Testament, and he agrees with writers like St. Paul and the author of the Fourth Gospel in regarding the possession of Divine life as a *present* possibility, and not something to be reached only in a new order of being, though he fails to reach their splendid vision of life eternal.

Nothing is more remarkable in this connection than his descriptions of what he conceives to be real death and real life, for he employs similar phraseology to that of St. Paul in similar discussions. "Natural death," he says, " is that in which the soul is separated from the body. But the death which is penal is constituted when the soul dies to the life of virtue, and lives only to that of vice" (*Leg. All.* i. 107). Cain's punishment he describes as "living in a continuous death, enduring, in a sense, a death which is immortal and endless. For there are two kinds of death. The one is the state of being dead, which may be good, or neither good nor bad (ἀδιάφορον); the other is the state of dying, which is altogether bad, and the more grievous to bear the longer it lasts" (*De Praem. et Poen.* 70). This passage shows that Philo draws a sharper distinction between physical and spiritual death than Paul does. When the Apostle speaks of death, he seems to regard the term synthetically, ignoring the common analysis into physical and spiritual, and regarding the dissolution of an existence which is out of touch with God as a single experience of ruin. In Philo's case the lot of mortality is overshadowed by the doom of the evil soul, which appears to him independent of time and space. An illuminating example of his

MAN'S YEARNING FOR GOD

position is found in *De Fuga*, 55. There he tells how reflection has taught him "that the worthless, although they reach extreme old age, are dead, for they are cut off from the life of goodness; while the good, even if parted from their union with the body, live for ever, sharing in a lot which is immortal." Here he stands in line with the Pauline view, that severance from the earthly body can never quench the life that is rooted in God.

Hence, Philo emphasises the endowment of the soul with eternal life, apart from the division of experience into present and future. "When the immortal type of being arises in the soul, the mortal forthwith suffers destruction. For the origination of worthy pursuits means the death of those that are base; since, when the light has once shone, the darkness disappears" (*Quod Deus sit immut.* 123). This is the counterpart in Philo of St. Paul's great antithesis between "dying to sin" and "living to righteousness," the first condition invariably leading on to the second. It is worthy of note that Philo attempts to define immortality from this precise standpoint. "This,"

MAN'S YEARNING FOR GOD

he declares, "is the finest definition of immortal life—to be possessed with a [fleshless and bodiless]¹ passion and friendship for God" (*De Fuga*, 58). Evidently it is such a relationship which purifies the soul. For in commenting on Gen. xv. 15, where it is said of Abraham, "Thou shalt *depart* to thy fathers in peace," he speaks of Scripture as here indicating "that the good man does not die, but departs, that it might declare the inextinguishable and immortal nature of the fully purified soul, which shall experience a departure from this world to heaven, not that dissolution and destruction which death appears to bring" (*Quis Rer. Div. H.* 276).

This passage prepares us for a more popular picture of immortality, again reminding us vividly of St. Paul, who also combines the more pictorial with the profounder idea. "When Abraham," he says, "left the mortal state, 'he was gathered to the people of God' (Gen. xxv. 8: Philo's own adaptation of the text), reaping immortality, made like unto the angels" (*De Sacrif. Ab.*

¹ Omitted by Cohn.

MAN'S YEARNING FOR GOD

et C. 5). It is almost needless to recall the startling parallel to the last clause in Luke's account of Jesus' answer to the Sadducees (Luke xx. 36). Similarly, having described the path of the soul towards goodness as ending in life and immortality, while that towards evil issues in the shunning of these blessings and in death, he remarks that "the God who loves to give, plants in the soul a kind of paradise of virtues and of the deeds which accord with them, which brings it to perfect bliss" (*De Plant.* 37). Occasionally, it is not easy to determine whether Philo's language on the destinies of souls is to be taken literally or metaphorically. Thus, in a fine passage (*De Somn.* i. 151 f.), he tells how "the wise have received an abode in the Olympian and heavenly region, having learned ever to sojourn above, while the wicked dwell in the recesses of Hades, having from first to last made it their aim to die, and from childhood to old age being accustomed to destruction." Possibly, however, the clause that follows regarding lives of laborious effort (ἀσκηταί), "which go frequently upwards and downwards as on a ladder, either drawn upward by the worthier lot, or pulled in the contrary direction by the less worthy," indicates that the metaphorical sense is uppermost in his mind. It is, however, noteworthy that Philo can deliberately speak of the ideal (νοητός) or spiritual world in remarkably concrete terms—terms which his master, Plato, would have shrunk from using. In conceiving it as the abode of immortality, he sets it in sharp contrast with the visible order as "a veritable world of intelligent beings" (Bréhier, *op. cit.* p. 240). Thus, in a classification of men, the highest place is taken by "men of God, priests and prophets, who had no ambition . . . to become citizens of the world, but reaching beyond the entire sensible universe, removed into the spiritual and dwelt there, enrolled in the commonwealth of immortal and incorporeal ideas" (*De Gig.* 61). The closing words remind us of his unfailing effort to fuse Hellenism with Jewish conceptions.

We have in the foregoing paragraph suggested various interesting comparisons with

MAN'S YEARNING FOR GOD

St. Paul. Yet the fact cannot be ignored that Philo's conception of immortality is far less rich in content than that of the Apostle. This is partly due to his failure to connect the Hope in any definite fashion with the consummation of the Kingdom of God and those spacious moral processes of the Divine government of the world which find their climax there. It is surrounded by too rarefied an atmosphere, philosophical rather than religious. And thus, while it strives to express, as we have seen, a genuine religious need, its undue intellectualism narrows it down to something less impressive even than the Apocalyptic conception of immortality.[1]

[1] In these paragraphs I am specially indebted for valuable hints to my friend Dr. J. H. Leckie.

CHAPTER V

GOD'S APPROACH TO MAN

(a) *The Grace of God*

IN our discussion of Philo's view of Faith, we found that it meant a complete turning away from the life of sense and the fixing of the soul's gaze upon God alone. This he regards as a supreme achievement of the spiritual life. But it presupposes an experience of the Divine working which is really the basis of its existence. Side by side with those abstract descriptions of God, which lay the emphasis on His incomprehensibility, and deny to Him as pure Being the possession of any qualities (ἄποιος), Philo reveals his place in the true succession of Old Testament piety by the prominence he assigns in the history of the soul's progress to the energies of the Divine Grace. Such

GOD'S APPROACH TO MAN

prominence is in no sense accidental. From the readiness with which his conviction of Grace is introduced as something self-evident to the religious mind, and the feelings of wonder and joy which it calls forth, it obviously belongs to the inmost texture of his devout experience. And it forms one of the many testimonies which his works supply that, in spite of his zeal for cosmological and psychological speculations after the model of his Greek masters, the crucial elements in his view of God and man belong to the spiritual heritage of his race. He does not attempt in any theoretical fashion, not even to the extent that Paul did, to divide the ground in this mysterious realm between God and man. He is content to accept as one of the most inspiring factors in the relation of God to His creatures the unceasing outflow of a Divine purpose of mercy, initiating all that is good in human life and opening up the highest possibilities to those who are conscious of nothing but imperfection.

This fundamental idea comes out in one of

GOD'S APPROACH TO MAN

those ingenious verbal distinctions to which he is so strongly addicted. Again and again he refers the difference between the two leading names given in the Old Testament to the Existent (τὸ ὄν), namely, "God" (θεός) and "Lord" (κύριος), to that between His two chief powers, the power of showing grace (χαριστική, e.g. *De Somn.* i. 163) or benefiting (εὐεργετίς, e.g. *De Spec. Leg.* i. 307), and that of exercising rule, which includes punishing (βασιλική, *De Somn.*, *loc. cit.* : κολαστήριος, *De Spec. Leg.*, *loc. cit.*), often summed up in the contrasted terms "beneficent goodness" and "authority" (ἀγαθότης and ἐξουσία, e.g. *De Cherub.* 27). The details in these discussions are often far-fetched, but his essential view emerges quite clearly. Each of these aspects of the Divine Being, which are combined in the Logos (*De Cherub.* 27), is to be acknowledged with reverence, but the "older" is that of beneficence. In speaking of the sinners of the Patriarchal age, he observes that, while many individuals perished, God, "in order that the human race might continue, mingles mercy [with judgment], using it to benefit even the unworthy; and not only does he show mercy after judging, but before judging he has mercy; for mercy is older with him [*i.e.* prior in his thought] than penalty" (*Quod Deus sit immut.* 76). How firmly rooted this conception is, appears from a fine passage (*De Plant.* 89), where he interprets the phrase "everlasting God" (Gen. xxi. 33) as "him who does not bestow grace at one time and withhold it at another, but is always and continuously the doer of kindness without interruption . . . who omits no opportunity of benefiting, while at the same time he is Lord, with the power also to hurt." So inherent to God is the bestowing of kindness, that even in the case of those who have committed intolerable wrongs, He desires to have intercession made to Him on their behalf (*De Mut. Nom.* 129).

The Divine Grace is conceived by our author on the most spacious lines. Expanding the words, "as for me, behold my covenant is with them" (Gen. xvii. 4), he says: "There are many different kinds of covenant which

GOD'S APPROACH TO MAN

bestow gracious benefits and gifts on those worthy of them, but I myself am the highest kind. . . . I myself am the source and fountain of all experiences of grace. For to some God is wont to extend his benefits by means of other channels, earth, water, air, sun, moon, heaven, and other incorporeal powers, but to others through himself alone, declaring himself the portion of those who receive him " (*De Mut. Nom.* 58 f.). All that exists, in so far as it can benefit, is an expression of the loving-kindness of God, imparted freely to all His creatures. And so if one were to ask, What is the principle ($ἀρχή$) of the created universe, the most accurate answer would be, the kindness ($ἀγαθότης$) and grace of God (*Leg. Alleg.* iii. 78).

But of supreme importance for human beings is the recognition that their own highest faculties are Divine gifts. Philo, as we know, regards man's spiritual nature in its supreme aspects as the in-breathing of the breath of God, and, in a very real sense, Conscience is, in his view, the energy of the Divine Logos actually present in the soul.

GOD'S APPROACH TO MAN

"God," he declares, in a passage highly relevant to our present discussion, "because of his gentleness and love for men, desiring to establish a shrine amongst us, found none on earth more fitting than our reason" (*De Virtut.* 188). But he is always sensitive to the actual situation. Man, with his power of self-determination, has misused his capacities. In his shallowness of judgment he has been allured by the superficial attractions of the sense-life, especially by pleasure, which has directed his strivings towards unworthy aims. In this situation the grace of God shines forth in all its splendour. "God, who is a lover of giving (φιλόδωρος, one of his favourite epithets for God), bestows his blessings freely on all, even on the imperfect, summoning them to follow eagerly after virtue" (*Leg. All.* i. 34). Men's condition puts the loving-kindness of God to a severe test. But God's grace and mercy go far beyond the standard of mere justice. His beneficent power is all-pervasive (*De Vita Mos.* ii. (iii.) 238). The fitting penalty for the human race, because of its ingratitude towards Him, its Saviour and

Benefactor, would have been annihilation; but He, by reason of His gracious nature, took pity and moderated their punishment (*De Op. M.* 169). His purpose for men is wholly good. He can, indeed, visit with calamity, but it is His special property to hold out blessings and to be beforehand with His gifts. Nay, even when penalty is deserved, God does not straightway visit it upon the sinner, but gives time for repentance and for the healing and amendment of his fault (*Leg. All.* iii. 105 f.). In a word, His aim is nothing less than the redemption of men. The Father, who has begotten the soul, does not desire to leave it for ever imprisoned, but, in His pity, to loose its bonds and conduct it safely in its freedom even to its mother-city, and not to cease until the promises of His words are ratified by actual deeds (*De Somn.* i. 181).

But at this point we are inevitably confronted by the perennial problem of the relation of the Divine Grace to human effort. Philo has no systematic treatment of the question, yet it is important to examine his

GOD'S APPROACH TO MAN

general attitude towards the facts. To begin with, he is clear that all goodness in the soul is due to the Divine operation. " It befits God to plant and build up the virtues in the soul : egoistic and impious is the mind which imagines itself equal to God, and presumes to be acting while it is really acted upon" (*Leg. All.* i. 48 f.) ; "what soul ever succeeded in putting out of sight and annihilating evil, save that to which God was revealed, which he deemed worthy of his ineffable mysteries?" (*ibid.* iii. 27). The progress of the soul, from its beginnings, depends on God's self-manifestation. In this whole province there is a remarkable parallelism between Philo and St. Paul. A most notable example of the position which they may almost be said to occupy in common appears in *De Migr. Abr.* 30 ff. : "The fountain from which blessings stream is our communion (σύνοδος) with God who loves to give : this is why he puts the seal upon his benefits by saying, I will be with thee. What good thing, then, could be lacking, when God who never fails of achievement is present, with

GOD'S APPROACH TO MAN

the virgin-powers of his grace ? In that case effort and toil and hard exertion are stilled, and all that can benefit is imparted in abundance. . . . The mind lets go its hold of those energies which are at the command of its own designs, and is, as it were, liberated from its purposes by reason of the gifts rained upon it in unceasing showers." The context, indeed, suggests that this description applies primarily to the inward wrestling of the soul with truth. But since in Philo no valid distinction can be drawn between this search and the personal yearning after God, it seems legitimate to emphasise the striking resemblance to Paul as regards the cessation of human effort and the complete dependence of the soul on Divine aid. The position is confirmed by such statements as *De Mut. Nom.* 138: "There are few whose ears are open to receive these sacred words which teach that it belongs to God alone to sow and to create (γεννᾶν) what is good."

Sufficient evidence has been adduced to show that Paul's great watchword: " By grace are ye saved, through faith, and that

GOD'S APPROACH TO MAN

not of yourselves, God's is the gift" (Eph. ii. 8), can be rendered directly in terms of Philo's thought, if we discount the Apostle's definitely Christian background. Precisely as in Paul's view, Philo regards man as having nothing in which he can glory in God's presence. Even anything good which he achieves—and Philo, like Paul, recognises the importance of such achievement—must ultimately be ascribed to Divine influence. For it is impossible for a human creature to rid himself of his defilement. "What period would suffice to wash away these stains? I cannot tell. . . . What eternity could transform the impurity of a soul into a well-ordered life? Not even an eternity, but God alone, to whom are possible the things which with us are impossible" (*De Spec. Leg.* i. 281 f.). The words have an extraordinary affinity with New Testament positions. If we may regard them as expressing an undertone of religious feeling beginning to appear in the more enlightened Judaism of the Diaspora, we are indeed moving in an atmosphere in which the way of the Lord is being prepared.

GOD'S APPROACH TO MAN

Now, the clause, "through faith," in Paul's famous utterance, states the human condition of the saving process. God's gift of grace must not be mechanically conceived. The manner of the Divine activity is not to force an entrance into any heart. Apart from a free and glad assent of the soul, that which Paul calls Faith, there can be no real contact between the grace of God and human need. Philo, from his own standpoint, frankly acknowledges this. He has various ways of describing the condition of receptiveness to which the Divine generosity can make its appeal. Once and again he finds the condition fulfilled in the *suppliant* attitude of the soul. "When pleasure," he says, "loses its power, and the cause of our shocking and wanton life has in a sense died, we weep over and deplore our former career, because we preferred pleasure to virtue and linked a mortal to an immortal life. Then the only Gracious, taking pity on our unbroken confusion, draws near to our suppliant souls" (*Quod det. pot.* 95). Similarly, "God will perform the work which belongs to him,

GOD'S APPROACH TO MAN

having proclaimed release and freedom to the souls which supplicate him" (*Quis Rer. Div. H.* 273). Often, in this connection, it is the reaction from an unworthy life, the recoil of the soul, which affords its opportunity to the grace of God. "When God is gracious," says Philo, "he makes all things easy [reading ἐξευμαρίζει with Cohn]. Now he becomes gracious to those who feel shame and exchange dissoluteness for self-control and reproach a culpable life and loathe the base phantoms which they impressed upon their souls, who are eager for the quieting of passions and haste after calm and peace of life" (*De Praem. et Poen.* 116). So, too, in an important passage (*De Somn.* i. 9), which we quoted in discussing Repentance, he emphasises the grace of Him, who alone is gracious, to those who lay bare their hidden thoughts and deeds, which are already exposed to the glance of the Father of all.

There are certain aspects of the Divine Grace which are singled out by Philo. That which we first note has an arresting kinship with the New Testament outlook. "Very

GOD'S APPROACH TO MAN

aptly [Moses says that] their supplication reached God. Now it would not have reached, if he who invited it had not been gracious. But some souls he goes out to meet: 'I will come to thee and will bless thee' (Ex. xx. 24). You see how large is the grace of the Cause, who anticipates our hesitation and goes out to bestow the completest benefits upon the soul" (*Leg. Alleg.* iii. 215). Here we are not merely reminded of Paul but of Jesus Himself, and especially of the marvellous delineation of the Father in the parable of the Lost Son. Indeed, Philo shows himself of the lineage of the great prophet Hosea in his emphasis on the unwearying ardour of the Divine pity. God is the Shepherd of the Soul. His "watchful oversight is . . . the first and only reason why the parts of the soul are never left without attendance but find a blameless and unfailing good Shepherd" (*De Agric.* 49 f.). There is, in short, in the nature of God no limit to the outflow of His generosity towards men. More than once this affluence of the Divine bounty provokes in Philo an outburst of

GOD'S APPROACH TO MAN

praise. "O thou Lover of giving," he exclaims, "without stint are the gifts of thy grace, having no limits or boundaries or end, like fountains which pour forth streams too plentiful to be borne away" (*Quis Rer. Div. H.* 31). The only limit to the grace of God lies in the narrowness of men's capacity to receive it. Thus Philo lays down as the normative principle for human beneficence that which God imposes upon Himself because of human limitations: "Freely give not all that thou canst, but all that the needy is able to receive" (*De Post. Cain.* 142). "For that which has come into being," he observes in the same passage (*ibid.* 145), " is never without a share of God's gracious gifts ... but is unable to bear their abundant and lavish current. Wherefore, desiring us to be profited by his bounties, he measures them according to the capacity of the recipients." Philo enlarges on the theme in dealing with Moses' prayer (Ex. xxxiii. 13 f.) for a vision of God, and the Divine answer to his request. " I freely bestow that which befits him who is to receive: for not

GOD'S APPROACH TO MAN

all that I might easily give is it possible for man to take. Therefore I hold forth to him who is worthy of my grace all the gifts he is able to receive. But for a complete apprehension of me there is no room, not only in human nature, but even in all earth and heaven. Know thyself, then, and be not carried away by impulses and desires beyond thy powers . . . for in all attainable good thou shalt have a share" (*De Spec. Leg.* i. 43 f.). One further aspect of Philo's view of Divine Grace may be pointed out before we leave this phase of our discussion. It is important, because it reminds us that Philo, so far from being absorbed merely in theoretical inquiries, has his gaze firmly fixed on the higher claims of practical life. He is laying stress on the proper use of the gifts, often unexpected, which men receive from God. "For," he says, "the generous bounties of the Supreme Ruler, which he bestows on individuals, are for the general well-being: not that when they have received them they may hide them or misuse them to the hurt of others, but that, putting them into the

GOD'S APPROACH TO MAN

common stock, as at a public feast, they may invite as many as they can to their use and enjoyment" (*De Virtut.* 169).

(*b*) *Mediation*

The statments we have collected from Philo to illustrate his conception of the Grace of God are remarkable for their directness, simplicity, and freedom from technical phraseology. That is thoroughly characteristic of the man. When he discloses the profoundest realities of his religion, he usually lays aside metaphysical and psychological arguments. But recognising, as we must, the constant emphasis he places upon the transcendence of God, and his invariable assumption that the Existent cannot come into direct contact with the world of created things, we are not surprised to find the idea of Mediation between God and man at the heart of his thought.

The philosophical drift of his age, which affected most of the serious thinkers on religion in the centuries immediately preceding and following the birth of Jesus, favoured this

GOD'S APPROACH TO MAN

doctrine. The Ideas of Plato, and the λόγοι σπερματικοί (generative rational forces) of the Stoics, both of which played so prominent a part in the later philosophy, were already conceived, especially in the more popular philosophical theology, as powers in a sense mediating between the Absolute God or the First Cause and the universe. Parallel movements may be traced in every direction. The Stoics themselves had, by means of allegory, used the popular mythology to establish the idea of subordinate spiritual powers which were manifestations to men of the Divine. The Hellenised theology of Egypt had, on similar allegorical lines, attempted to combine the myth of a creative Word with the Divine Reason pervading all things. And the Hermetic literature, also of Egyptian origin, makes Hermes, who represents the Egyptian Thoth—the amanuensis of the gods, the god of all wisdom, who has invented "the words of God" (*i.e.* the written characters)—the bearer of a Divine revelation which he communicates to disciples that they may diffuse it abroad.

GOD'S APPROACH TO MAN

It may be said without undue rashness that Philo must have come into touch with all these various currents of thought. But he was exposed to others at least as important proceeding from his ancestral Jewish faith. The Alexandrian *Wisdom of Solomon*, written not long before his time, reveals the place given in cultivated Jewish minds to Wisdom, conceived almost as a Divine personality, subordinate to God, but "a breath of the power of God," "an image of his goodness," which "has power to do all things," "renews all things," and "entering consecrated souls makes them friends of God and prophets, for God loves none but him who is in fellowship with wisdom" (*Wisd.* vii. 25 ff.). But while we know this conception to have been influential in Philo's immediate environment, the idea of mediation between God and the world had taken further shape in Jewish religion. A prominent figure in Old Testament tradition was that of the "angel" or "messenger" of Jahweh, through whom the Divine mind and purpose was disclosed to men. Angelology had been developed to an

GOD'S APPROACH TO MAN

extraordinary extent within Judaism between the Exile and Philo's time, perhaps chiefly under the influence of Babylon and Persia; and the stress laid upon the Holiness of God in the post-exilic community gave an impetus to a large number of personifications of the Divine. The actual evidence for some of these belongs to a period later than Philo. But when we take into account their Old Testament basis, and remember that by his time the transcendence of God was a dominating idea both in Palestinian and Alexandrian Judaism, it is in no way improbable that he was acquainted with them at some stage in their evolution. Thus, the Rabbinic hypostasis of Memra, the Creative Word of God, has its roots in passages of Genesis (*e.g.* i. 3, 6, 9) and Psalms (*e.g.* cxlvii. 15) which describe the efficacy of the Divine utterance. The Shekinah, which is a sort of concrete embodiment of the Divine Presence, represents, of course, the "glory" of Jahweh, described in the Old Testament as filling the Tabernacle and the Temple. Ezekiel's complex vision (chap. i.) became a favourite subject

GOD'S APPROACH TO MAN

of speculation in various circles of Judaism, and the winged creatures which bore the moving throne of the Almighty were explained as the powers of God. But from the description of the vision, the living creatures might be viewed as a unity, as well as in their individuality. When so regarded, the unified appearance, of which the several faces were aspects, was named in esoteric Judaism "the charioteer." It is impossible to avoid the supposition that Philo was directly influenced by this group of speculations, when he designates the Logos "charioteer of the Divine powers" (*De Fuga*, 101). Further, as Siegfried has cogently pointed out (*Philo von Alexandria*, p. 221 f.), the dignity of the High Priest had been immensely enhanced in the post-exilic community, so that to a degree never before conceived he stood as mediator between God and the people. The efficacy of his suppliant prayers is emphasised in several Rabbinic treatises, and also his intimacy with the All-Holy. A striking comment on the fact is Philo's ascription of the title "High Priest" to the Logos (e.g. *De*

GOD'S APPROACH TO MAN

Fuga, 108 ff.; *De Migr. Abr.* 102). And it is probably legitimate to regard this as one of the factors which set the Priesthood of Christ in the centre of the Epistle to the Hebrews, a document whose Alexandrian and Philonic associations are evident throughout.

Philo's attempts to bridge the gulf which he assumes between a God who is pure Being and the world of Becoming circle round the conception of the *Logos*, who is God's Thought or Reason; the *powers* (δυνάμεις) of God, which are manifestations of His energy, operating in the universe; and *angels*, a considerably vaguer category. It lies outside our purpose to discuss these categories in their metaphysical bearings. The Logos-hypothesis itself, as it appears in Philo, is full of confusion. This is no doubt partly due to its composition from heterogeneous elements, Platonic dualism, Stoic monism, and Jewish monotheism, modified by the later belief in hypostases of God, of which the most notable was Wisdom. In part, it depends on the fluctuating boundary in ancient thought

GOD'S APPROACH TO MAN

between personality and personification, and on Philo's own tendency to glide from what he conceived as truth to symbols of truth. To some extent it results from his failure in constructive power.

A few words on the cosmic significance of these Divine energies will serve as an introduction to their religious functions as suggested by Philo. Probably his most inclusive description of the Logos in this realm is that of "the ideal world," "the image of God," the pattern according to which the perceptible universe has been fashioned (e.g. *De Op. M.* 24 f.). As the Logos is the "image" of God, so *par excellence* is human reason the "image" of the Logos (e.g. *Leg. Alleg.* iii. 96). Not only has the Logos been God's instrument (ὄργανον) in creation, but he is, so to speak, the "helm" (οἴαξ) by which the Almighty Steersman pilots the universe (*De Migr. Abr.* 6). A metaphor which he is fond of applying to the Logos is that of the Divine seal, by which each created thing is stamped and receives its permanent quality (*De Fuga*, 12 f.). Varying the details of the comparison, he

GOD'S APPROACH TO MAN

speaks of the rational soul as stamped by the seal of God, whose impression is the eternal Logos (*De Plant.* 18). Roughly speaking, these descriptions tally with the conception of the Thought of God, more or less abstracted from His pure Being, and placed beside Him in a semi-personified form.

Philo usually conceives the powers as subordinate to the Logos. Thus he speaks of God as having completely filled His Divine Logos with incorporeal powers (*De Somn.* i. 62). But perhaps the clearest instance is *Qu. in Exod.* ii. 68 (p. 515, Aucher), where in discussing the relation of the two primary Divine "powers," the gracious creative power (θεός) and the regal (κύριος), to the Logos, he speaks of these as "flowing out from the Logos as from a spring," and then proceeds to show how other powers emanate from them. These Powers, which he classifies variously (e.g. *Legat. ad Gaium*, 6, 7), and of which we have just mentioned the most representative, he describes as stretched from the roots of the earth to the confines of heaven, holding together the entire universe

GOD'S APPROACH TO MAN

(*De Migr. Abr.* 181). As in the case of the Logos, he so objectifies the Powers as over against God, that their inferiority is clearly manifest. Thus God uses them for the punishment of sin, a function unseemly for Himself. They were His instruments in creating the mortal elements of the soul, as contrasted with the rational. In some sense, also, they are responsible for the presence of conceptions of evil as well as of good in the human soul (*De Fuga*, 66 ff.).

Let us now turn to the more practical aspects of these mediating agencies, which give them an important place in the religious and moral experiences of the soul. Bréhier (*op. cit.* p. 100) is true to the facts when he observes that in order to understand the real position of the Logos in Philo, we must leave on one side philosophical and cosmological theories and consider God and the Logos as objects of worship. In the progress of the soul towards the Highest, the apprehension of the Logos is an intermediate stage which must be passed through. "It is a boon," Philo says, "for perishable mortals to have medi-

GOD'S APPROACH TO MAN

ating and arbitrating Logoi (*i.e.* rational Divine powers), because of their own awe and shrinking before the Lord of all" (*De Somn.* i. 142). This is no mere dread of punishment. It means their incapacity to receive God's overpowering and unmixed blessings, when these are given by His own hand (*ibid.* 143). In these paragraphs we are face to face with a characteristic standpoint of post-exilic Judaism. "God can only be grasped by means of the powers which accompany and follow him. For these do not present his essence but only his existence, to be gathered from what is accomplished by him" (*De Post. Cain.* 169). In distinguishing between the two instances of the word "place" in Gen. xxii. 3 f., Philo remarks that "the man who is under the guidance of wisdom arrives at the first two places mentioned, having found the Divine Logos who is the crown and goal of satisfaction" (*De Somn.* i. 66), and a few sentences later he speaks of the Logos as sent forth to heal and completely cure the ailments of the soul. Perhaps the most fundamental passage for his general working conception is

GOD'S APPROACH TO MAN

Quis Rer. Div. H. 205: " The Father, who has begotten all things, granted as his choicest privilege to his chief messenger and most august Logos, that he should stand in the midst between the Creator and the created. Now he is, on the one hand, always the suppliant for transient mortals in presence of the Immortal, and the ambassador of the Ruler to his subject. Thus he rejoices because of the privilege, and prides himself on it . . . being neither uncreated like God nor created like you, but standing between the two extremes as a pledge to both, to him who created as an assurance that created beings will never wholly rebel or revolt, choosing confusion rather than order, and in the case of the creature to give him the bright hope that the gracious God will never ignore his own work." This remarkable utterance reaches the heart of Philo's conception of the Logos. What has further to be said is simply an expansion of its ideas in various directions.

It will not help us much to discuss, in the light of such statements, how far Philo regards

GOD'S APPROACH TO MAN

the Logos as in some sense, a " personality," distinct from God, whose Thought or Reason or Utterance he is. We have already referred to the vagueness of the boundary in ancient thought between personality and personification. In the New Testament precisely the same problem arises; as, *e.g.*, in the Pauline Epistles with reference to the relation between the Spirit and the exalted Lord. And it is needless to recall the numerous controversies in the early Church which sprang directly out of this region. Philosophical or religious thinkers, in attempting to make any affirmations at all within the realm of spirit, are compelled to formulate such distinctions, although reflection at once reminds them that they are working with anthropomorphic categories, and that this picture-language must be recognised for what it is, an inadequate effort to express the inexpressible. Philo is no more and no less successful in his efforts than Christian theologies or idealistic philosophies. But it can scarcely be doubted that his particular differentiation of the Logos from the Supreme

GOD'S APPROACH TO MAN

God had an exceptional influence on the subsequent Christology of the Church.

Philo gives prominence to the idea that those mediators, whether Logos, δυνάμεις, or ἄγγελοι, come to the soul's assistance in all its higher aspirations. "He who follows after God," he says, "has . . . as companions on his journey those rational powers (λόγοι) who accompany God, who are commonly called angels. . . . For as long as he is not perfected, he has the Divine Logos to show him the way. . . . But when he has reached the summit of knowledge, having run eagerly he will equal in swiftness him who formerly led the way. For both will become attendants of the omnipotent God" (*De Migr. Abr.* 173 ff.). Indeed he implies that their very function is to consider and aid the spiritual needs of man. "For help," he observes, "a succouring power waits in readiness in God's presence, and the Ruler himself draws nearer for the benefit of such as are worthy of receiving benefits" (*ibid.* 57). In the passage already quoted as specially typical, the Logos is described as "a suppliant for transient mortals." This is an aspect which occurs more than once.[1] And we cannot help finding traces of its influence in the primary place assigned in "Hebrews" to the work of intercession in the priesthood of Christ.

In one important place (*De Confus. Ling.* 146) God's "first-born Logos" is described as "a being of many names." We shall glance at some of these, from the point of view of religious significance. Commenting on Gen. xliii. 11 (LXX), Philo asks: "How could you hesitate, my friends, to hate war and love peace, you who are called by the name of the same father, not a mortal but an immortal, a Divine man, who, being the Logos of the Eternal, is himself necessarily imperishable?" (*De. Conf. Ling.* 41). Now, whatever shade of meaning may have been here attached to the term Logos in Philo's

---

[1] We entirely disagree with Drummond's position, that "in all these passages we are concerned only with certain functions of human reason and speech," and that the term ἱκέτης excludes any idea of intercession (*Philo Judaeus*, ii. 236, 235). The latter statement seems quite arbitrary when viewed in the light of the context of these passages. And to us it appears that no statements in Philo more clearly suggest the idea of personality than those in question.

GOD'S APPROACH TO MAN

mind: whether the idea of the Divine Reason in man predominates, or that of a vicegerent of the Eternal, who bridges the chasm between the seen and the unseen, it is plain that such a usage must lead even unconsciously to the personalising of the conception. We can never determine what point in the process has been reached, but the more powerfully the notion of religious value is present, the more concrete will be the shape which the Logos idea assumes. An illuminating instance of how the various *nuances* of the term shade off into each other appears in *De Somn.* i. 103 ff. Philo begins by observing that Logos, obviously in the sense of "reason," but sometimes gliding into that of "speech," is God's choicest gift to man, his "bulwark," his "bodyguard," his "protagonist," the power that "furthers his aspirations." He is the "saving remedy for the passions of the soul," a "counsellor and champion" whose presence gives joy and rest. But at the close of the passage, all that has been affirmed is merged in the figure of the "Divine Logos," whom the

GOD'S APPROACH TO MAN

ascetic soul, renouncing itself, "awaits as a visitant coming invisibly from without." All through the paragraph we are inevitably reminded of the New Testament conception of the indwelling Spirit, which often can scarcely be distinguished from the renewed nature of the Christian, but at other times is viewed quite separately. Such a distinction appears plainly in *De Somn.* i. 86: "The Logos of God when he visits our earthly system of things helps and succours those who have kinship with goodness and tend in that direction (cf. John iii. 21), so as to provide for them a complete refuge and salvation, but on the enemies of good he launches ruin and incurable destruction." Here the Logos is set over against God and men as the representative of the Eternal, acting for men's highest well-being. Once, in a discussion of the incomprehensibility of the Divine Nature, the "Logos-interpreter" (cf. John i. 18) receives the remarkable appellation "God of the imperfect," as opposed to the Eternal, who is God "of the wise and perfect" (*Leg. Alleg.* iii. 207), a class which,

GOD'S APPROACH TO MAN

probably for Philo as for the Stoics, remained no more than an ideal. Perhaps nowhere is the religious colour of the Logos-conception more visible than when he describes it, quite incidentally, as "the heavenly, incorruptible food of the soul that longs for the vision of God" (*Quis Rer. Div. H.* 79), or when he compares it to a river. "As from the fountain of wisdom, the Divine Logos flows down to refresh and water the Olympian and heavenly plants of souls that love goodness, a kind of Paradise." This is "the river of God, full of water," referred to in Ps. lxv. 9, "a stream of wisdom, which makes glad the city of God" (Ps. xlvi. 5), "the soul of the wise, in which God is said to walk to and fro as in a city" (*De Somn.* ii. 242 ff.).

We have barely mentioned the important fact that Philo sometimes identifies the Logos with Wisdom. Referring, *e.g.*, to "goodness" as the genuine virtue, he declares that its source is the wisdom of God. "That," he adds, "is the Logos of God" (*Leg. Alleg.* i. 65). This identification cannot surprise us, as Philo was, of course, familiar with the

GOD'S APPROACH TO MAN

commanding place occupied by the hypostasis of "Wisdom" in the deeper thought of his Jewish contemporaries. It is possibly true that Greek influence accounts for the overshadowing of the latter conception by the former in his writings. But this influence may have been indirect rather than immediate in his case, inasmuch as the term Logos, as a mediating idea, covered a far wider range of relations than Sophia, and thus more adequately met the needs of his thinking. So far as their range is the same, the parallelism could scarcely be closer, and we cannot help believing that Philo's own extension of the application of Logos in certain directions was made possible by his acquaintance with the mediating function of Sophia in the Wisdom-literature of the Jews. One special use of Logos, although possessing affinities with that of Wisdom, may perhaps be traced more directly to his Egyptian environment, in which Divine "words" were endowed with unique potency. In a few passages he uses it to describe the all-efficacious utterance of God. Thus, in referring

GOD'S APPROACH TO MAN

to the account of Moses' death in Deut. xxxiv., where it is ascribed (ver. 5) to the "word of the Lord," he says by that "word the whole universe was created, that you may learn that God counts the wise man of equal value with the world, by the same Logos both producing the totality of things, and leading the perfect man from his earthly environment to himself" (*De Sacr. Ab. et C.* 8). This and other instances are, however, isolated from the main trend of his usage, and he goes out of his way to assert that the Divine utterance has no point of comparison with the human (*Quod Deus sit immut.* 82 f.), thus preserving for it its fundamental significance of the ideal form which brings coherence into the universe. Yet we can easily understand how, in spite of this, a Jewish mind, accustomed from the Old Testament to the idea of God's all-powerful Word, might find in Philo's usage a significance which the author himself had barely suggested. That would be all the more likely if he were already sensitive to those personifications of the Divine Wisdom which represented her as

GOD'S APPROACH TO MAN

pleading with men and offering them instruction in the name of God (*e.g.* Prov. viii. and ix.).

We must bear all these considerations in mind when we place beside Philo's conception of the Logos that which belongs to the Prologue of the Fourth Gospel. Dr. Rendel Harris, with remarkable skill and contagious enthusiasm, has tried to prove that the writer is entirely dependent on the Sophia of the Wisdom-literature, and he works out the influence of this conception through one and another of the Early Christian Fathers, as well as in St. Paul. No doubt he has succeeded in unravelling one strand of a variegated pattern. But the other threads must not be ignored. The demonstration of many remarkable parallels to Sophia in the famous Prologue by no means excludes Alexandrian features, for these parallels certainly came within Philo's horizon. No conclusive argument has been as yet produced to account for the Fourth Evangelist's choice of Logos in preference to Sophia. And that choice, in the light of Philo's employment of the term,

GOD'S APPROACH TO MAN

affords a strong presumption in favour of Alexandrian affinities. The progress of research in Hellenistic thought, whether Jewish, Pagan, or Christian, continually puts us on our guard against the tendency to trace kinship along a single line. Syncretism is the sign-manual of the period. And Ephesus, the home of Heraclitus, with his conception of Logos as the "comprehensive principle of order in the unified world-process," was not likely to remain indifferent to the far-reaching developments of the idea, whether among the Stoics or in Philo. But one aspect of the question is not open to dispute. To Philo, as to any of his pagan contemporaries, it would have appeared an inversion of all values, whether religious or metaphysical, that the Evangelist should have dared the tremendous assertion: "The Logos became flesh, and dwelt·among us."

CHAPTER VI

UNION WITH GOD

ALL careful readers of Philo must agree with the statement of Windisch, that "Religion is for him an inward impetus of the soul, a quest for and delight in Divine revelations, a craving after fellowship with God, an experience of God" (*Die Frömmigkeit Philos*, p. 80). How to attain communion with the Unseen is the question which absorbs his spirit. Now the very presuppositions of his thinking about human nature encourage him to press towards his goal. For if anything can be called fundamental in his view of the constitution of things, it is the conviction which he assigns to "those who have gone deep into the meaning of the laws" that "God gave man as the best of his gifts a share with himself in his rational nature" (*De Op. M.* 77).

UNION WITH GOD

Man starts, therefore, with a real kinship to God. It is inevitable that, in proportion as the Divine element asserts itself, he will strive after more complete union with the Fount of his being.

(a) *Fatherhood and Sonship*

In this connection it is worth while briefly to examine Philo's application of the categories of Fatherhood and Sonship to the relation between God and men, as that may shed some light on the background of the New Testament. He is fond of ascribing to God the name of "Father," and this under various aspects. By far the most fundamental of these is that of Creator. "The mind of the unseen," he says, "has begotten the whole: but the Creator is superior to the created. Hence he cannot be borne along in the inferior, apart from the unfitness of a father being contained in his son: rather must the son grow through the care of his father" (*De Migr. Abr.* 193). Similarly, in *De Cherub.* 49, God is named "Father of all" as "having begotten them."

UNION WITH GOD

We do not need to look for the origin of this conception, as some scholars have done, to the Platonic notion of "God" as Father of the universe. It is, of course, familiar from the Old Testament, *e.g.*, Deut. xxxii. 6: "Do ye thus requite the Lord. . . . Is not he thy father that formed thee? Hath he not made thee and established thee"; Mal. ii. 10: "Have we not all one father? Hath not God created us?" Isa. lxiv. 8: "But now, O Lord, thou art our father; we are the clay, and thou our potter; and we are all the work of thy hand."

We do not clearly understand what Principal Drummond means by saying that when Philo represents man as a "son" of God, he gives it an explanation "which reduces it to an ordinary figure of speech," and that "the term is used as a designation of spiritual worth, and is not connected with the ontological relations of man" (*Philo Judaeus*, ii. 281–282). Can it ever be fruitfully used in the province of religious thought except as "a designation of spiritual worth"? If we attempt to regard it under the category

UNION WITH GOD

of "ontological relations," can we arrive anywhere? Even Jesus, for whom the conception is so central, has no interest in "ontological relations." " Love your enemies," He enjoins upon His followers, "and pray for them that persecute you, that you may become sons of your Father who is in heaven" (Matt. v. 44 f.). This, surely, must be called "a designation of spiritual worth." Indeed, one of the most interesting passages in Philo bearing upon the subject has some affinities with that famous utterance. "Those," he says, "who act upon their knowledge of the One,"—a phrase explained in what follows as "estimating the noble alone to be good,"—"are fittingly called sons of God, as Moses also acknowledges in the words, 'ye are sons of the Lord God' (Deut. xiv. 1), and 'God who begat them' (Deut. xxxii. 18), and 'Is not this thy Father'" (*ibid.*) (*De Conf. Ling.* 145). But this he regards as a difficult achievement, to be reached by stages. Therefore he adds: " But even if a man be not yet actually worthy of being called a son of God, let him aim at

UNION WITH GOD

being ranked in that relation to the Logos, God's first-born son, the oldest of angelic beings" (*ibid.* 146). Like Jesus, Philo seeks to raise the mind from earthly to heavenly relationships. "Why should we remember only our human father? We have the uncreated, immortal, Eternal" (*De Jos.* 265). "The law," he says, "confirms my suggestion when it declares that those who do what is acceptable . . . and noble are sons of God, for it declares, Ye are sons of the Lord your God, obviously indicating that they are to be deemed worthy of such providence and solicitude as a father bestows. Now this care will differ as greatly from human care, I believe, as he who cares differs [from a human father]" (*De Spec. Leg.* i. 318). A very illuminating utterance, in view of the matter we have been discussing, is *Quaest. in Gen.* i. § 92 (p. 66, Aucher): "Sometimes, indeed, he [Moses] calls the angels sons of God, seeing that they were not made incorporeal by any mortal man, for they are spirits without bodies. But with preference that great teacher names sons of God the noblest of men, those endowed with

UNION WITH GOD

virtue." Here Philo makes his position plain, and it certainly approaches the standpoint of the New Testament. Recognising, then, that we can only interpret such a relationship ethically and spiritually, we find real religious significance in his comment on the well-known words of Gen. xviii. 17, "Shall I hide from Abraham my friend (τοῦ φίλου μου, not in known MSS of LXX)?" "He who possesses this portion has passed beyond the limits of human well-being: for he alone is high-born who can inscribe God as his Father and has become his only adopted son" (*De Sobr.* 56). It would be easy to trace the parallel between such an utterance and some of those in which St. Paul sets forth the unique privileges which belong to "adoption" in the Christian sense. We cannot describe a relation of this kind by any other term than "personal," and so, mainly in virtue of his Old Testament conception of God, Philo has something more intimate in view than the Stoics when they designated the "wise man" as a son of God. It is from this standpoint that he can speak

UNION WITH GOD

of "the Father and Saviour" as "having pity" on the soul that yearns to behold Him (*De Praem. et Poen.* 39). But while we have pointed out affinities in this realm of thought between Philo and the New Testament, we fully recognise that his tendency to resolve God into hypostases has detracted from the unity and power of an otherwise most impressive Theistic conception.[1]

(*b*) *The Spirit of God*

It comes natural to those who approach the great Jewish thinker from a New Testament point of view to ask what place he assigns to the Spirit of God in his analysis of the process by which the human soul strives to attain fellowship with the Divine. We have seen that he does recognise, although far less prominently than the New Testament writers who have caught the inspiration of Jesus, the possibility of a filial relation between man and God. Is this in any way associated, as in the New Testament, with a doctrine of

---
[1] See Windisch, *op. cit.* pp. 97, 98. On the background of πατήρ in Philo, see esp. J. Kroll, *op. cit.* pp. 30-32.

UNION WITH GOD

the Spirit? Or, does the conception of the Spirit exercise any important influence on Philo's idea of communion between the finite and the Infinite? We certainly cannot accept off-hand Dr. Bigg's unqualified statement that "the doctrine of the Holy Spirit . . . has no place in his system" (*Christian Platonists of Alexandria*, p. 25). The evidence fails to justify it. But an examination of the facts may bring out some interesting features of Philo's view.

One of his fundamental positions is that man could have formed no conception of God, had God not breathed into that part of his nature which was endowed with higher potentialities His own "breath" or "spirit" (πνεῦμα). Thus, he says, "there comes about a union (ἕνωσις) of the three," *i.e.* of God, the human νοῦς, and the Divine πνεῦμα (*Leg. Alleg.* i. 37 f.). This, of course, represents man's highest capacity, whether or not it be afterwards developed. It cannot be compared with the specifically Pauline use of πνεῦμα, but seems closely akin to what the Apostle calls νοῦς or ὁ ἔσω ἄνθρωπος. Its pre-

UNION WITH GOD

dominant characteristics appear to be rational. It is the essence of the "governing element" in human nature, and he identifies it with λογισμός, reason (*Quis Rer. Div. H.* 55 ff.). In another place he speaks in notable terms of the "rational soul" of man as "the genuine coinage of that Divine and invisible spirit, marked and stamped by the seal of God, whose impress is the eternal Logos" (*De Plant.* 18). That is to say, the rational element in the soul is the stamp on human nature of the Divine Spirit, the impress of the Logos, which cannot here be distinguished from the πνεῦμα of God. On the same lines, the Divine part of man, "the noblest aspect of the soul which is called νοῦς and λόγος, mind and reason," he designates by the general description of τὸ πνεῦμα (*Quod det. pot.* 83). In these instances we are not dealing with an attainment in the religious life, but with an original endowment. But in the most interesting and elaborate of all the passages in which he discusses the Divine Spirit, he reveals a wider outlook. Discussing the statement of Gen. vi. 3

UNION WITH GOD

(LXX) : " My spirit shall not dwell with men for ever, because they are flesh," he comments : " He does remain sometimes, but he does not dwell always with most of us. Who indeed is so irrational . . . as never either voluntarily or involuntarily to receive a notion (ἔννοιαν) of the Highest ? Nay, even over the reprobate there often hovers the impression (φαντασία) of the good, but they cannot grasp it and keep it by them. For it vanishes at once, turning away from those . . . who have abandoned law and right. Indeed, it would never have visited them, except to convict them sharply of preferring the base to the noble. Now, according to one usage, the air that rises from the earth is called Divine πνεῦμα . . . but according to another it means that pure (ἀκήρατος) knowledge in which every wise man fully shares." He proceeds to illustrate this aspect of the Divine Spirit by the special equipment of wisdom and understanding bestowed upon Bezaleel for the construction of the Tabernacle, and by the imparting to the seventy elders of the spirit of Moses,

UNION WITH GOD

which he describes as "wise, Divine, indivisible, noble, without any defect" (*De Gig.* 20 ff.).

Here he recognises a physical sense of πνεῦμα, equivalent to "air," which recalls Stoic descriptions of God as the "aëry essence" (οὐσία ἀεροειδής) which permeates all existence (e.g. *Diog. L.* vii. 148). Indeed, his language throughout this paragraph has various echoes of Stoicism, as when he speaks of "receiving a notion" (ἔννοιαν λαβεῖν) of God, and refers to the "impression" (φαντασία) of the good. And the influence of Platonic terminology is evident when he calls the Divine Spirit in its highest aspect "that pure knowledge in which every wise man shares."[1] But the passage shows that he is fully sensitive to the Old Testament conception of the Spirit as a Divine equipment, a Divine gift, an experience not to be identified with that natural endowment which he also calls the inbreathing of the πνεῦμα. Obviously it will be as a rule

[1] See *Phaedrus*, 247 D : διάνοια νῷ τε καὶ ἐπιστήμῃ ἀκηράτῳ τρεφομένη (so Bekker)

UNION WITH GOD

impossible to distinguish the Divine Spirit in this sense from the Logos. And in all likelihood the reason why the conception is not more prominent is just that the Logos absorbs its functions. But it is straining the evidence to say, as Zeller (followed by Drummond) does, that Philo only speaks of the Divine Spirit when the idea is presented to him by some text of Scripture (*Phil. d. Griechen*⁴, iii. 2. 2, p. 432, note 2). There is nothing artificial or awkward in his employment of the category. His most arresting references occur quite incidentally, and their basis is not theory but experience. "The invisible Spirit which is wont to commune with me unseen whispers to me and says" (*De Somn.* ii. 252). Here is an instance from his own life of fellowship with God. In another place he appears to include himself when he recounts what happens to "prophetic" natures: "The mind ($νοῦς$) in us departs at the coming of the Divine Spirit, and when it leaves, returns to its abode. For it is not fitting that mortal should dwell with immortal. Thus the sinking of reason

UNION WITH GOD

and the darkness which encompasses it beget ecstasy and God-inspired frenzy" (*Quis Rer. Div. H.* 265). In these passages, in which he speaks most intimately of the Divine Spirit, he is in no sense influenced by some direct reference in Scripture.

Further light is shed upon his conception by the references he makes to the conditions of the Spirit's indwelling. "Let us keep still from wrong-doing," he says, "in order that the Divine Spirit of wisdom may not easily remove and depart, but may abide with us for a long, long time, as with Moses the wise man" (*De Gig.* 47). It may be noted that in the context the "Spirit" is identified with ὀρθὸς λόγος, an identification common in Philo. In the same treatise (53) he declares that "among the majority," *i.e.* those who set before them many ends in life, the Divine Spirit does not abide, even if for a short time he may sojourn, but only with one type of men does he dwell, that which has stripped off all that belongs to the world of becoming, "and the inmost veil and curtain of opinion, and with unrestricted and open

UNION WITH GOD

mind reaches God." Moses is adduced as an example of this type, one "who enters into the darkness, the unseen place, and abides there while he is initiated into the most sacred mysteries. Indeed, not only does he become an initiate, but also a hierophant of mystic rites, a teacher of Divine things, in which he gives instruction to those whose ears have been purified. With such a man the Divine Spirit is ever present, showing him the way in every straight path" (*ibid.* 54 f.).

But while there is a real approximation in Philo's use of the conception of the Spirit of God to that in the New Testament, we not only feel that in his thought it is secondary, but also that as an energising power it is grasped with far less vigour and discerned in a dimmer light than, *e.g.*, by St. Paul. We have no doubt that for Philo also it represents the formulation of an experience, but that experience lacks the sureness and depth and permanence which characterise the Apostle's endowment. And the reason surely is that in Philo the Divine Spirit is one special de-

UNION WITH GOD

scription of a fluctuating and elusive category like the Logos, while St. Paul indissolubly associates it with that which has the most concrete reality for his spiritual life, the person and activity of the living Lord.

(c) *The Vision of God*

For Philo, the crowning achievement of the pious spirit is the Vision of God. "What lovelier or more fitting garland could be woven for the victorious soul than the power, with clear vision, to gaze upon Him who is? Truly splendid is the prize held out to the wrestling soul—to be equipped with eyesight so as to perceive without dimness Him who is alone worthy of contemplation" (*De Mut. Nom.* 82). That man has reached the heights of blessedness to whom it is granted not merely by knowledge to apprehend all that belongs to the natural order, but to behold the Father and Maker of the universe. For there is nothing higher than God: he that has succeeded in stretching his soul's vision as far as Him may well pray to abide there without change (*De Abr.* 58). For such

UNION WITH GOD

vision is no mere passing rapture. It must prove a singular aid in the good life. " If the sight of elders or instructors or rulers or parents move the beholders to reverence and orderly conduct and the desire for a self-controlled life, how great a bulwark of virtue and honourable living may we expect to find in souls which, reaching beyond all that is created, have been trained to behold the Uncreated and Divine " (*Leg. ad Gaium*, 5). This fundamental conviction lets us see into the heart of Philo's religious aspiration.

It is a good thing, he holds, for the soul to seek God. For even the striving after goodness brings a sort of preliminary satisfaction. But it is a matter of uncertainty whether the search will reach its goal. Many failed to attain. God did not reveal Himself to them (*Leg. All.* iii. 47). Here is the crux. The highest stage of religion, the only fully satisfying attainment, means revelation. Philo does not so much discuss the idea of revelation in itself as presuppose it in what he affirms concerning the spiritual vision of God. But in speaking of some whose

UNION WITH GOD

search is not fruitless, he describes God as " Himself, by reason of his gracious nature, going forth to meet them with his virgin-graces, and revealing himself to those who crave to behold him, not as he is—for that is impossible . . . but in so far as it was possible for a created nature to approach his incomprehensible power" (*De Fuga*, 141).

What, then, are the *conditions* in which the spirit can attain the Vision of God? Philo has much to say on this problem. We shall try to select some crucial examples of the position which he occupies. In a set of reflections on Gen. xv. 5, where he takes the words, "He [God] led him [Abraham] forth," in a spiritual sense, he proceeds: " The mind that is to be led forth and set at liberty must withdraw from all things, from bodily necessities, from the instruments of the senses, from sophistical reasonings, from plausible arguments, finally from itself. . . . For it is not possible for one who dwells in the body and among mortal men to have communion with God, but only for him whom God delivers out of his prison" (*Leg. All.*

UNION WITH GOD

iii. 41 f.). This conception appears in a specially impressive form in *Quod det. pot.* 158 f. : "Will you then assert, O senseless man, that if you are deprived of bodily and external advantages you cannot reach the vision of God? I tell you that in that event you will surely attain to it : for you must be released from the iron fetters of the body and from bodily concerns if you are to receive the vision of the Uncreated. . . . For it was when [Abraham] left his whole house that the Law says, 'God appeared to him' (Gen. xii. 7), showing that God distinctly appears to him who escapes from material things and retires into the incorporeal soul of this body of ours." Philo sheds light upon his position in distinguishing between God's manner of revealing Himself to corporeal souls and those which are bodiless. "To these souls which are incorporeal and worship him it is natural that he should appear as he is, talking as a friend with friends. But to those still in the body he resembles angels, not indeed altering his proper nature, for he cannot suffer change, but impressing upon them who behold him

UNION WITH GOD

the notion of a different shape, so that they suppose that this image is not a copy, but that what they see is the original itself." (*De Somn.* i. 232). Philo goes on to say that for the benefit of dull natures God has to be represented in Scripture by anthropomorphic descriptions, for in this way alone can they be disciplined. But the more accurate statement is that of Num. xxiii. 17 : "God is not as a man." Hence, to mortals, He must reveal Himself in angelic guise. And His angel, as found in Scripture, is really His "image," the Logos (*ibid.* 236 ff.). But while life in the thraldom of the body is an insuperable barrier to the undimmed vision of God, he does regard it as possible, as passages quoted above plainly indicate, for a soul which has completely detached itself from the hampering conditions of mortal existence (and this he also assumes as a possibility) even now to attain the goal of its yearnings. He can speak of minds so "completely purified" that the Lord of all, "silently, unseen, alone, sojourns with them," while "with the spirits of those who are still

UNION WITH GOD

being cleansed and have not yet completely washed away the stained and defiled life they have lived in burdensome bodies, angels may dwell, Divine Logoi, making them bright and pure by the doctrines of high virtue" (*ibid.* 148). Abraham, the wise man, the stable soul, is the true pattern for those who would commune with God. "For in very deed only the unchanging soul can draw near to the unchanging God, and the soul in such a condition veritably stands beside the Divine power" (*De Post. Cain.* 27).

Now the purified soul has a certain *élan* or urge towards the beatific vision. "When the eyes formed of corruptible material reach so far as from the region of earth to scan remote heaven and touch its limits, how spacious must we suppose to be the sweep of the eyes of the soul! For these, winged by an eager longing to behold the Existent in his radiance, not only stretch to the utmost ether, but, passing beyond the bounds of the entire universe, hasten to the Uncreated." These are the souls which cannot be satiated with wisdom and knowledge. They are said to be "sum-

UNION WITH GOD

moned up" to God. "For it is meet that these should be called up to the Divine, who have been inspired by him." Thus it is by the Divine Spirit that the νοῦς is lightened and lifted up to the highest heights (*De Plant.* 22 ff.: cf. the fine description of a similar experience in *De Spec. Leg.* i. 207).

Let us try to ascertain how Philo conceives the Vision of God to be attained. We have seen that a presupposition of the achievement is the liberation of the mind or spirit from bodily entanglements and all material complications. It has, in a sense, to withdraw from the body in order to reach the Uncreated. Further, as a matter of experience it is only a few who reach the goal. But this small number are "so mighty in energy that not even the whole round of earth can contain them, and they reach heaven; for, possessed by an unquenchable longing to behold and to be ever in fellowship with the Divine, when they have closely investigated and scrutinised the whole of visible nature, they go at once in quest of the incorporeal, ideal world, taking none of

UNION WITH GOD

the senses with them, but leaving behind all that is irrational in the soul, and only making use of that which is called mind and reason" (*De Praem. et Poen.* 26). It is important to note that in all that Philo says of what is plainly an "ecstatic" experience, he makes the "rational" capacity of man the chief human factor. But even the purified human spirit is unfit to pursue this arduous quest alone. "There is danger for the soul in ascending to the vision of the Existent by itself, for it knows not the way, and may be puffed up by ignorance and rashness. . . . Wherefore Moses prays that he may have the guidance of God himself for the path that leads to him, for he says, Unless Thou go with me, take me not up hence" (*De Migr. Abr.* 170 f.). God Himself, therefore, comes to the aid of the yearning soul. He will assist its pursuit of Him. This is exemplified in the experience of Abraham. When his understanding had dispelled the mists of sense which confused it, he was scarcely able to grasp, as in clear air, the impression of the Unseen. But God, "by

UNION WITH GOD

reason of his philanthropy, did not turn away from the soul as it came to him, but going forth to meet it, revealed his own nature, in so far as it was possible for the beholder to see it. Hence it is said, not that the wise man *saw* God, but that God *appeared* to the wise man. For it was impossible that any one should grasp by himself the truly Existent, unless he had manifested and revealed himself" (*De Abr.* 79 f.).

What, then, is Philo's conception of the Vision? It need scarcely be said, in view of statements already discussed, that contradictory utterances are to be found. "When the soul that loves God searches into the nature of the Existent, according to his essence, it enters into an unseen and invisible search, from which the chief benefit that accrues to it is to comprehend that God is incomprehensible and to see that he is invisible" (*De Post. Cain.* 15). The classical instance is the experience of Moses as narrated in Ex. xxxiii. 13 ff. All that is vouchsafed to him is a vision of the environment of the Divinity. "His nature does

UNION WITH GOD

not admit of being seen: and what wonder that the Existent cannot be grasped by man, since even the mind in each of us is unknowable by us. For who ever beheld the essence of his soul?" (*De Mut. Nom.* 9 f.). Yet very important statements occur of an opposite drift. And these probably bring us as near as we can reach to an analysis of a mystical experience which is really beyond analysis. "There is," he says, "a more perfect and more completely purified type of spirit [again exemplified by Moses], initiated into the Divine mysteries, which does not reach a knowledge of the First Cause from created things, of the substance, as it were, from the shadow, but overleaping the created, receives a clear manifestation of the Uncreated, so as to *grasp Him from Himself*" (*Leg. All.* iii. 100). Some light is shed upon the meaning of this vague phrase by several remarkable utterances. Describing the discipline of the wrestling soul, Philo speaks of a point at which "a bright incorporeal ray, purer than ether, suddenly shining upon it, revealed the ideal world as under guidance. But the

UNION WITH GOD

Guide, encompassed by unstained light, was hard to behold or to divine, for the soul's vision was obscured by the splendour of the rays. Yet she, despite the streaming towards her of intense radiance, endured, through her extraordinary craving for a vision. Then the Father and Saviour, seeing her genuine longing and yearning, pitied her, and imparting power to the approach of her sight, did not withhold the vision of himself, in so far as it was possible for a created and mortal nature to contain it" (*De Praem. et Poen.* 37 ff.). He seems to feel, however, that his description is quite inadequate. And so he returns to the experience. "How this approach [*i.e.* of the eyes of the soul to God] has taken place, it is worth while observing *by means of a simile.* Can we behold this sense-perceived sun by any other means than the sun itself? Or, can we behold the stars by any other means than the stars? In a word, is not light seen by means of light? In the same fashion God also, who is his own radiance, is seen through himself alone, no other co-operating,

UNION WITH GOD

or being able to co-operate towards the pure apprehension of his existence" (*ibid.* 45). We may connect with this a noteworthy statement in *Qu. in Gen.* iv. § 1 (p. 238, Aucher): "Since God is incomprehensible, not only to the race of men, but also to all the parts of heaven which surpass men in purity, he caused a certain radiance to flash forth from himself, which we may rightly call his form, scattering incorporeal rays about the mind and filling it with super-celestial light. Under this guidance the mind is led, through the mediating form, to the Prototype."

Some further clues to the meaning of what he conceives as the most intimate experience of union with God may be found in certain descriptions of moments of spiritual rapture. And first let us recall his famous account of his own spiritual illumination as a thinker. "I am not ashamed," he says, "to recount my own experience. . . . At times, when I proposed to enter upon my wonted task of writing on philosophical doctrines, with an exact knowledge of the

UNION WITH GOD

materials which were to be put together, I have had to leave off without any work accomplished, finding my mind barren and fruitless, and upbraiding it for its self-complacency, while startled at the might of the Existent, in whose power it lies to open and close the wombs of the soul. But at other times, when I had come empty, all of a sudden I was filled with thoughts showered down and sown upon me unseen from above, so that by Divine possession I fell into a rapture and became ignorant of everything, the place, those present, myself, what was spoken or written. For I received a stream of interpretation [reading, with Markland, ἔσχον γὰρ ἑρμηνείας ῥεῦσιν], a fruition of light, the most clear-cut sharpness of vision, the most vividly distinct view of the matter before me, such as might be received through the eyes from the most luminous presentation" (*De Migr. Abr.* 34 f.). Such illumining of his spirit means for him the direct impact of the Divine. And no doubt it has contributed materials

UNION WITH GOD

to his attempt, acknowledged by himself as inadequate, to delineate the soul's vision of God. Of similar import is his remarkable appeal to the soul in *Quis Rer. Div. H.* 69 f.: "If a yearning come upon thee, O soul, to possess Divine blessings, forsake not only thy 'land,' the body, and thy 'kindred,' the life of sense, and thy 'father's house' (Gen. xii. 1), the [uttered] word,[1] but escape from thyself also, and go forth from (ἔκστηθι) thyself, filled with a Divine frenzy like those possessed in the mystic rites of the Corybantes, and holden by the Deity after the manner of prophetic inspiration. For when the mind is filled with God and is no longer self-contained, but rapt and frenzied with a heavenly passion and driven by the Truly Existent and drawn upwards to him, while truth goes in front and removes obstacles that it may tread the highway,— this is thy [Divine] inheritance." Here is an impressive description of spiritual ecstasy, and perhaps it delineates with as much de-

[1] See *De Migr. Abr.* 2: λόγον τοῦ κατὰ προφοράν, a passage which explains the symbolism here.

UNION WITH GOD

finiteness as Philo could reach what for him, on the basis of real experience, was the content of his most intimate union with God. He makes a like appeal in *Quaestt. in Exod.* ii. § 51 (pp. 505–506, Aucher), in which, after laying down certain conditions, the cutting off of desires, pleasures, despondencies, fears, and the casting aside of folly, wrong-doing, and cognate evils, he shows the soul how it may be consecrated to God a living temple. " Then he may appear to thee visibly, causing incorporeal rays to shine upon thee, granting visions of his nature undreamed of and ineffable, which are the overflowing sources of all other blessings." In such experiences it is plain, as Bréhier fitly expresses it, that " Philo's contemplation [of God] is . . . an inward rapture in which all precise knowledge disappears in the feeling of the existence of a Being incomprehensible and without limitations" (*op. cit.* p. 296). Here we inevitably recall the parallel experience of a nature at various points so closely akin to that of Philo, although so immeasurably his superior in creative power.

UNION WITH GOD

St. Paul also has entered into the mystic ecstasy: "I knew a man in Christ who fourteen years ago was caught up to the third heaven. In the body or out of the body? That I do not know: God knows. I simply know that, in the body or out of the body (God knows which), this man was caught up to paradise and heard sacred secrets, which no human lips can repeat. Of an experience like that I am prepared to boast, but not of myself personally—not except as regards my weaknesses!" (2 Cor. xii 3 ff.: Moffatt's tr.). The smallest reflection will show that, like Philo, Paul feels himself rapt by the Divine power, his soul perfectly passive, and thus laid open for the reception of ineffable Divine revelations.

Attention has been already called to Philo's opposing statements regarding the possibility of an *immediate* apprehension of God, statements which have their parallels in the writings of many mystics. Possibly he is quite aware of these apparently contradictory standpoints. And some important utterances on the more and the less direct vision of the Existent

UNION WITH GOD

may be an attempt to suggest a *via media.* Of special significance is that in *De Abr.* 119 ff., a section in which he explains the symbolic meaning of Abraham's three heavenly visitants (Gen. xvii. 1 ff.). "When the soul, as at broad noon, is encompassed by the Divine radiance, and, being wholly filled with spiritual light, welcomes [reading αὐγὰς ἀσπάσηται, with Wendland] the rays poured forth around, it receives a threefold impression of the one essence, the first as of One who is three, the other two as of shadows cast by him. . . . Let no one, however, suppose that we can properly speak of shadows in the case of God. We only use this expression to bring out more clearly what has to be explained. . . . But, as one might say in close accord with the truth, the Father of all stands in the midst, who in Holy Scripture is called by his proper name, the Existent, while on either side are his highest Powers, those closest to the Existent, the creative and the ruling. . . . With these, then, as his attendants, He in the midst presents to the spirit that has vision at one time

UNION WITH GOD

the impression of one, at another of three; of one, when the mind is in the highest state of purification and not only passing beyond the multitude of numbers, but also beyond the Two which is the neighbour of the One, hastens to the unmixed and uncompounded Idea, which needs no other than itself; of three, when the mind has not yet been initiated into the Great Mysteries, but still only knows the lower grades, and cannot grasp the Existent *from himself alone* without the help of another, but only through what he does, either as creating or ruling." This paragraph is full of interest as indicating how Philo attempted to satisfy his own mind as to the relation of the mediate to the immediate vision of God. The spirit which is "in the highest state of purification" is that which is able fully to renounce itself and to yield wholly to the Divine influence. Not that Philo appears ever to adopt the conception, characteristic of mysticism, of a complete fusion of the individual soul with God. But its self-consciousness is suppressed, and, as in prophetic inspiration, which seems power-

UNION WITH GOD

fully to have influenced his conception, it becomes simply the receptacle or the instrument of the Divine Spirit.

Thus the two poles of thought stand over against each other. On the one hand, the transcendent God cannot be grasped by finite creatures. Yet no other goal will satisfy. Perhaps, as Zeller suggests (*Philos. d. Griechen*[4], iii. 2. 2, p. 463), "the very transcendence of Philo's conception of God arose, not from the attempt to cut off all relations between men and God, but rather from the very opposite effort, to reach the Deity, whom he could not find in himself or in the world, beyond the bounds of all finite existence." That could only be realised in a Divinely inspired ecstasy, in which the finite, for the moment, transcended mortal limits, and was virtually endowed with infinity.

CHAPTER VII

THE MYSTICISM OF PHILO

WE have attempted in the preceding chapter to give a brief description of what Philo means by the soul's Vision of God, that which he conceives to be the supreme spiritual attainment. This attainment, we found, is realised in an ecstatic condition in which the restrictions of sense are for the moment left behind, and the purified soul is alone with the Alone. But Philo's Mysticism, which reaches its crowning point in this high experience, has so large a bearing upon his whole religious outlook and aspirations that it calls for a more detailed examination.

It has already been noted that success in the quest after union with God is regarded by Philo as the meed only of a few. This conviction colours both his thought and his

THE MYSTICISM OF PHILO

language. Again and again when he deals with the ineffable discoveries of the soul in God which he seeks to elucidate allegorically, he speaks as if to an esoteric circle, and employs the terminology of the Mystery-cults of paganism. "This," he exclaims, "receive in your souls, ye initiates, purified of hearing, as veritably sacred mysteries, and divulge it not to any of the uninitiated, but keep it in the storehouse of your mind as a treasure not composed of silver and gold, substances which perish, but as the fairest of existing possessions" (*De Cherub.* 48). The same awe in declaring the deeper secrets of the Divine appears in *De Sacr. Ab. et Cain.* 60, where he speaks of the necessity of hiding "the sacred revelation concerning the Uncreated and his Powers, since not every one can guard the deposit of the Divine ritual." Moses' action in pitching the tabernacle (which the LXX of Ex. xxx. 7 calls "his tent," and Philo "his own tent") outside and away from the camp, means that "having established his mind firmly, he begins to worship God, and having entered into the cloud abides there,

THE MYSTICISM OF PHILO

receiving initiation into the Divine Mysteries. Indeed he becomes not only an initiate but also a hierophant of ritual and a teacher of Divine things, in which he guides those whose hearing is purified " (*De Gig.* 54). The full force of this mystic terminology is made clear by *Leg. All.* iii. 100 : " There is a more perfect and purified type of spirit which has been initiated into the Great Mysteries, which does not discover the Cause from created things, the abiding, as it were, from the shadow, but overleaping the created, receives a clear vision of the Uncreated so as to apprehend him from himself"[1] Possibly this usage requires no further explanation. In every period, those whose spiritual affinities are mystical draw together through the attraction of a common experience and cultivate on its basis a common speech. Yet there is something to be said for Reitzenstein's hypothesis (*Poimandres*, p. 204, note 1) that Philo was here influenced by his Egyptian environment in which there had grown up as the result of

---

[1] See the interesting collection of mystery-terms from Philo in Bousset, *Religion d. Judentums*², p. 519, note 3.

THE MYSTICISM OF PHILO

mystery-cults "an elaborated literary form and manner" of this type. That is, however, something very different from the theory which accompanies it, that Philo's doctrine of ecstasy is itself the product of Hellenistic religion, a question to which we must return.

Before we go further, let us try to form some more or less clear notion of the terms we have to use. Mysticism, it need scarcely be said, is one of the most question-begging descriptions of certain elusive because very personal spiritual conditions. Some powerful minds regard such states as a kind of narcotic indulgence of the sensibilities, fostered by turbid thought and unethical feeling. Some at the opposite extreme would embrace under the name those experiences which are supremely life-enhancing. Others associate it with individualities of a religious bent whose intellectual nature is completely overshadowed by the emotional. And further interpretations of "Mysticism" have been current. Hence there has come into vogue a use of the term as lax as that of such words as "evolution," "realism," "socialism."

THE MYSTICISM OF PHILO

It is surely true, as Dr. Bigg suggests, that "in one sense all believers in the unseen are mystics" (*Christian Platonists of Alexandria*, p. 99, note 1) That is to say, a stage may be reached in the experience of communion with God which is so intimate as to be indescribable in terms of normal states of consciousness. Various degrees of intensity may be discovered in the attitude of the spirit which, to use Plotinus' phrase, is "in love with" God. Probably some spiritual minds which delight in exercising a strong control over the processes of their Godward aspiration discredit the circle of ideas usually called "mystic," because to them it seems to imply spheres of being that are nebulous or morally unproductive. Yet many such persons would willingly admit that St. Paul stands on the summit of religious experience when he exclaims : " I have been crucified with Christ: nevertheless I live; yet not I, but Christ lives in me: indeed the life which I now live as a man I live by faith—faith in the Son of God, who loved me, and gave himself for me " (Gal. ii. 19, 20). But faith in Paul's profound

THE MYSTICISM OF PHILO

sense of the term undoubtedly involves a mystical element, a factor or condition which eludes psychological analysis, although it is far removed from many of the typical formulations of what may be called technical mysticism. On the other hand, there have been yearning souls throughout the ages whose dominant aim has been to get beyond the limits of self and to be merged in Him who is the All. This probably represents the most intensified degree of the mystical experience in the strictest sense. It is, however, in reality no more than the exaggeration of an element which is discernible everywhere in religious experience, by whatever designation it may be named, the longing for union with the Divine. This is described from the standpoint of his own special experience by St. Paul as being "in Christ": and from a totally divergent angle of vision by an entirely different type of thinker, Spinoza, as *amor intellectualis Dei*.[1] The goal in all cases is

---

[1] But, as Mr. C. C. J. Webb cogently points out, "there is in this *amor intellectualis Dei* no question of *reciprocation*" (*God and Personality*, p. 70).

THE MYSTICISM OF PHILO

complete unification of life. For some this means individuality raised to its highest power, for others entire absorption in Perfect or Absolute Being.

There can be little doubt that the direction which this *mystical* element in human nature is trained to take, depends largely on the temperament of the individual. Many will be content to satisfy its needs in the relation which Faith in its deep Pauline sense establishes between the soul and God. For such, no abandonment of personality is involved. Rather does personality reach for the first time its full realisation. Others, however, are led to discipline their spiritual natures so resolutely by patient concentration on the goal of their desires that they enter upon abnormal spiritual conditions of greater or less intensity which assume the nature of a trance. This state also may vary indefinitely. Its most common form is ecstasy. "Taken alone," says Miss Underhill, "and apart from its content, ecstasy carries no guarantee of spiritual value. It merely indicates the presence of certain abnormal psycho-physical conditions, an alteration of the normal equilibrium. . . . Ecstasy, physically considered, may occur in any person in whom (1) the threshold of consciousness is exceptionally mobile, and (2) there is a tendency to dwell upon one governing idea or intuition. Its worth depends entirely on the objective worth of that idea or intuition." (*Mysticism*, p. 430). It need scarcely be said that the governing idea in the case of all truly mystical natures is that of God.

The excellent summary of the facts just quoted will serve as an introduction to an examination of Philo's mysticism. And it also puts us on our guard against a misconception which has recently gained currency through the dogmatic assertions of prominent scholars. Thus Reitzenstein declares that Philo's doctrine of ecstasy is "to be fully explained from Hellenism," and, quoting certain commonplaces of mystical technique, remarks that "Philo has taken over these Hellenistic theories" (*op. cit*. p. 204, note 1, 238, note 3). Similarly Bréhier attempts to

THE MYSTICISM OF PHILO

show that various mystical doctrines in Philo have their origin in traditions of Egyptian mystical theology such as are to be found in Plutarch's treatise, *On Isis*,[1] and the *Hermetic Tractates* (see esp. *op. cit.* pp. 245-248). Apart altogether from the fact that these tractates are of much later date than Philo, and must have been as directly exposed to his influence as we know Plotinus to have been, the material he adduces is in no sense the special property of Egyptian theology. Still less are the mystic conceptions which Reitzenstein (followed as usual by Bousset) finds him to have borrowed from his environment in any degree characteristically Hellenistic. They bear the familiar stamp of Mysticism as it appears in every quarter of the world where spiritual or even unspiritual religion is cultivated. To describe the invariable phenomena of the mystic quest for God as the peculiar product of Hellenistic religious activity, is to ignore a realm of facts

[1] It is plain to the careful reader of such texts as *De Cherub*. 42 ff. and *Leg. All.* iii. 3, 139, quoted by Bréhier in support of his view, that Philo's use of earlier ideas in these passages is purely metaphorical and illustrative.

THE MYSTICISM OF PHILO

of which no one who writes on the history of religion has any business to be ignorant.

We have recognised how frequently Philo uses the terminology of the Mystery-cults of paganism for his own purposes. His actual estimate of these cults is made sufficiently plain by such passages as *De Spec. Leg.* i. 319: "Further, he (Moses) removes from the sacred legislation rites and mysteries and all such clap-trap and buffoonery, considering that people brought up in such a commonwealth as Israel are above cultivating ritual and despising truth and running after ceremonies belonging to the darkness of night, while they cling to mystic fictions and ignore what can stand the light of day. Therefore let none of Moses' disciples and friends either initiate or be initiated. For either of the two, the teaching or learning of mystic rites is no small profanation. . . . Let those whose activities are hurtful be ashamed and search for holes and recesses in the earth and deep darkness, and let them hide and cast a shadow over their own unrighteousness. . . . Ought we not openly to

THE MYSTICISM OF PHILO

offer whatever is needful and profitable to all who are worthy of it for their benefit? But the fact is that seldom is a good man initiated, but you do find robbers and pirates and bands of wretched, unbridled women, because they pay fees to the hierophants who initiate them."

Let us more minutely scrutinise that condition of ecstasy or inspiration in which Philo, like most mystics, attains his most satisfying apprehension of the living reality of God. How completely his thought is saturated with ecstatic experiences appears from his constant use of the vocabulary of Divine possession. Terms like ἐνθουσιασμός, "Divine inspiration," ἐνθουσιάζειν, "to be Divinely inspired," ἐπιθειασμός, "Divine rapture," ἐπιθειάζειν, "to be in a condition of Divine rapture," κορυβαντιᾶν, "to be filled with supernatural frenzy," βακχεύειν, "to be seized with Divine madness," κατέχεσθαι "to be possessed by Deity," κατοκωχή, "Divine possession," θεοφόρητος, "possessed by God," and its corresponding verb, θεοφορεῖσθαι, ἔρως οὐράνιος, "heavenly passion,"

THE MYSTICISM OF PHILO

and ἔκστασις, "ecstasy," are of frequent occurrence.[1] It is unnecessary to enlarge on the fact established in our last chapter that the literal meaning of the word "ecstasy" is fundamental for Philo. We there quoted a passage of marked significance (*Quis Rer. Div. H.* 69 f.) in which he adjures the soul that craves the *summum bonum* of the Beatific Vision to "escape from" (ἀπόδραθι) itself, to "go forth from" (ἔκστηθι) itself, "filled with a Divine frenzy like those possessed in the mystic rites of the Corybantes." This association of ecstasy with an inward rapture is found repeatedly in Philo. A very important instance is *Leg. All.* i. 82 ff. "When the spirit (which allegorically represents Judah, ὁ ἐξομολογητικός, the man given to praising God") goes out of itself and offers itself to God . . . it there and then surrenders (ὁμολογίαν ποιεῖται, possibly, 'comes to terms with') to the Existent. . . . And truly it must be observed that this act of praise (τὸ ἐξομολογεῖσθαι) is not the doing of the soul

---

[1] See the useful list in Bousset, *Religion d. Judentums*², p. 517, note 2, which might be considerably extended.

THE MYSTICISM OF PHILO

but of God, who reveals to it his beneficence." The passage occurs in a paragraph in which he compares the various tribes of Israel to the jewels in the high priest's breastplate. Judah, the symbol of the man who praises God, has as his gem the carbuncle (ἄνθραξ). For the spirit which he represents, the spirit which goes out of itself, "is kindled into a flame of thanksgiving to God and becomes drunken with that drunkenness which does not intoxicate." Again, in an interpretation of the story of Hannah who was rebuked for drunkenness (1 Sam. i. 14) as she prayed before the Lord, Philo remarks: "In the case of the God-possessed not only is the soul wont to be stirred and driven into frenzy, but to be flushed and inflamed, since the joy which wells up within and makes the spirit glow transmits the experience to the outward parts" (*De Ebriet.* 147). Very suggestive is an actual description of ecstasy (*Leg. All.* ii. 31). Taking as his basis Gen. ii. 21 (LXX), "God put Adam into a trance (ἔκστασις) and caused him to sleep," Philo says that "the going-forth (ἔκστασις) and

THE MYSTICISM OF PHILO

turning (τροπή) of the spirit is a sleep which falls upon it. It goes forth when it ceases to busy itself with the ideas which impinge upon it, and when it does not exercise activity upon them it slumbers. Its going forth is an apt account of what happens, that is, its turning in the direction not of itself but of God who . . . imparts to it this new direction." In this definition of ecstasy the emphasis is placed not on the rousing of the spirit to a Divine madness, but on its quiescence. And this aspect of the condition appears to be as familiar to Philo as the other. We have referred in a former chapter to that experience of the soul which he calls "intercourse with the God who loves to give," in which there is a cessation of all effort, and the soul simply receives the Divine bounties (*De Migr. Abr.* 30 f.). He delineates the beginnings of the Quietist type of ecstasy with real vividness in *Quaestt. in Gen.* iv. 140 (Aucher, pp. 350–351), where he is discussing Isaac's solitary meditation in the fields at the close of the day. "The man," he says, "who highly values the

THE MYSTICISM OF PHILO

removal and absence of all thought of the visible, begins to lead a solitary life alone with the sole invisible God. . . . Hence, nominally, they go forth from their city or home; really, the meaning is that the spirit, apart from the body (*per se*), begins to be inwardly so inspired and initiated in Divine things as to be possessed almost wholly by God." Some other utterances are sharper in outline. "The most secure method of contemplating (θεωρεῖν) the Existent is with the soul alone, apart from all utterance" (*De Gig.* 52). Dean Inge, who points out that the ecstasy of Plotinus was of this calm type which is experienced in solitude, remarks that "the vision of the One is only the highest and deepest kind of prayer, which is the mystical art *par excellence*" (*Philosophy of Plotinus*, ii. p. 143). In the light of his statement it is worthy of note that Philo gives no prominence to the conception of prayer as the request for blessings from God. Indeed, he contrasts such request with what he calls "great prayer" (basing the expression on Num. vi. 2), namely, the conviction that

THE MYSTICISM OF PHILO

"God is of himself the cause of blessings, without the co-operation of any one else" (*Quod Deus sit immut.* 87).

A careful reader of Philo can scarcely avoid the conclusion that, so far from conceiving ecstasy in terms of Hellenistic religion, the thought in which he endeavours to express the mystic experience is determined by the phenomena of prophetic vision in the Old Testament. The prophet is above all else a man of piercing glance, "having within himself a spiritual sun and unshadowed rays so as to grasp with perfect clearness those things invisible to the senses and only to be apprehended by the mind" (*De Spec. Leg.* iv. 192). These prophetic functions, indeed, may be caricatured. And here, no doubt, he has in view the "prophets" who are influential among his pagan contemporaries. Those who deal in divination parody the Divine possession of the genuine seer. "Each by his guesses and conjectures sets forth an order of things out of harmony with truth: and easily cajoling the unstable in character, like a stiff blast blowing against

THE MYSTICISM OF PHILO

ships without ballast, retards and capsizes them and prevents them from reaching the sacred havens of piety. For he deems it his duty to proclaim his divinations not as inventions of his own, but as Divine oracles imparted to him alone in secret, in order to gain a surer confidence for his deceit from large companies of people. Such a man he [Moses] designates by the accurate name of false prophet" (*De Spec. Leg.* iv. 50). In contrast with him the genuine prophet "declares nothing at all of his own, but is an interpreter of the promptings of another in all that he proclaims, continuing in a state of ignorance all the time he is Divinely possessed: for his reason has removed and withdrawn from the citadel of the soul, where has come to dwell the Divine Spirit, stimulating and producing sound in the entire mechanism of the voice so as clearly to reveal that which he predicts" (*ibid.* 49 : cf. the exact parallel, *ibid.* i. 66). We may note in passing the further light shed by the contrast on Philo's estimate of the Hellenistic idea of possession. And the account of the true

THE MYSTICISM OF PHILO

prophetic state reminds us of the material which this Jew of Alexandria contributed to the formation in the early Church of a rigid doctrine of inspiration. More than once he singles out as central for the prophetic state the falling into abeyance of reason (νοῦς) which is confined within definite limits of comprehension, and its replacement by the Divine influence which opens up for the prophet a new realm of vision (e.g. *De Vita M.* ii. 6).

But perhaps the clearest exposition of his conception is to be found in *Quis Rer. Div. H.* 249 ff., a passage which shows that he has reflected carefully on these abnormal phenomena. Here he distinguishes four types of ecstasy. The first he describes as "a mad frenzy which produces derangement in old age or melancholia or some such symptom." The second is "the intense stupor caused by events happening suddenly and unexpectedly." The third is "the quiescence of the understanding when at any time it comes to be still." The fourth, "the noblest type of all, is that Divine possession

THE MYSTICISM OF PHILO

and frenzy characteristic of prophetic natures." This experience is typical of the inspired man. But Philo has a wider view of the possibilities. "Holy Scripture," he says, "allows prophecy to every fine and noble nature. For the prophet sets forth nothing of his own but what lies beyond his range, at the prompting of another. Now it is not right for a worthless person to become the interpreter of God. Therefore, properly speaking, no rascal is divinely possessed. This befits the wise alone: for he only is the echoing instrument of God, invisibly struck by him. Hence all whom he [Moses] recorded as righteous he introduced as possessed and exercising prophetic functions." He proceeds minutely to analyse the ecstatic state of the prophet, taking as his starting-point the words of Gen. xv. 12: "About the setting of the sun, ecstasy fell upon him." "As long as our own reason encompasses us with brightness . . . filling our whole soul, as it were, with noonday light, we remain in ourselves and do not experience possession. But when the light of reason sets . . . ecstasy

THE MYSTICISM OF PHILO

and Divine possession and frenzy fall upon us. For when the Divine light blazes forth, the human sets, and when that sets, this rises. That is what is wont to happen to prophetic natures. For the reason within us leaves its abode at the arrival of the Divine Spirit, but when the Spirit departs the reason returns to its place. For it is not fitting that the mortal should dwell with the immortal. On this account the setting of the rational power and its obscuration produces ecstasy and inspired frenzy. And what accompanies this he weaves into the text of Scripture, saying (Gen. xv. 13), 'it was said to Abraham.' For truly the prophet, even when he appears to speak, is really silent, while another uses his organs of speech, his mouth and tongue, to declare his will."

The fundamental element, therefore, in ecstasy as conceived by Philo, is the replacing of the human reason (νοῦς or λογισμός) by the Divine Spirit, which takes complete possession of the personality and uses it for its own high ends. An interesting passage

THE MYSTICISM OF PHILO

(*Quaestt. in Gen.* iii. 9) adds one or two features to his main conception. Ecstasy is there described as a "Divine excess made tranquil," and emphasis is laid on the fact that it does not come on gradually, but with a sudden inrush of the Spirit. Possibly, however, this latter statement must be estimated in the light of his view as a whole. For, as we pointed out in an earlier chapter, Philo is often influenced in the precise formulation of his thought at any given time by the actual words of the text on which he is commenting. And here the text (Gen. xv. 12) reads : " An ecstasy *fell upon* Abraham." The earlier part of the description recalls the existence of ecstatic states in which frenzy has no part. One specially pregnant instance of this negative aspect of the condition ought not to be omitted. In a symbolic interpretation of Ex. xxxii. 27, where Moses commands the members of the tribe of Levi, who have remained loyal to God, to attack the worshippers of the golden calf, and to slay "each man his brother and his neighbour, and him who is nearest to him," Philo takes

THE MYSTICISM OF PHILO

the first class mentioned as representing the body, which is the *brother* of the soul; the second, as standing for the material element, which is the *neighbour* of the rational; and the third, as signifying the "uttered Word," which stands *nearest* to the mind. "For only thus," he says, "could the noblest element in us worship the noblest of all existences if, in the first place, the man were reduced to soul, its brother the body with all its ineffectual desires being disjoined and separated from it: if, secondly, the soul, as I remarked, should cast aside the irrational element, the neighbour of the rational— for that, like a torrent divided into five parts among the five senses ... stirs up the current of the passions—if, in the next place, the reason should divorce and separate from itself the uttered word, so that the rational should be left alone, parted from the body, parted from the sense-life, parted from the sound of the uttered word. For when thus left to live a life of solitude, it can cleave to the only Existent in purity and without being drawn aside" (*De Fuga*, 90 ff.). This

THE MYSTICISM OF PHILO

remarkable passage lays bare the bed-rock of Philo's conception of ecstasy as that uninterrupted stillness of the soul, that complete unity of being in which no discordant element exists, and God can reveal Himself without let or hindrance. It prepares us directly for what is perhaps the highest description in his writings of the issue of prophetic inspiration, expressed in his answer to the question: " Why does Scripture say, Moses alone shall draw near unto God?" (*Quaestt. in Exod.* ii. 29). "This," he observes, "is said perfectly naturally. For the prophetic mind, when it has been initiated in Divine things and is inspired, resembles unity.[1] . . . Now he who cleaves to the nature of unity is said to have approached God with the intimacy as it were of a kinsman. For, abandoning all mortal types, he is transferred into the Divine type so that he becomes akin to God and truly Divine."

---

[1] This has reference to certain numerical speculations on Moses and his companions, Aaron, Nadab and Abihu (§ 27), in which Moses is represented by the first numeral 1, symbolising the purest intelligence, the prophetic, while the other three are adornments of that.

THE MYSTICISM OF PHILO

In ecstasy, therefore, the spirit reaches the true end of its being, the pure apprehension of God. "For the goal of bliss is the advent of God who draws near, bountifully filling the entire soul with all his incorporeal and eternal light" (*Quaestt. in Gen.* iv. 4 ; Aucher, p. 246). In this condition it desires to remain. For if the visitation of God be only transient, the soul is left forlorn and empty : in a moment thick darkness comes upon it (*ibid.*, *loc. cit.*). And yet the passing of this blissful experience is inevitable. It is not possible for a created being uninterruptedly to sustain the Divine presence (*deum in se gerere* : *ibid.* 29; Aucher, p. 268). "When the spirit, possessed by the love of God, reaching to the very holy of holies, advances with all eagerness and ardour, it forgets all else in its Divine rapture : it forgets even itself, and remembers and cleaves to Him alone whom it attends and worships, to whom it solemnly dedicates its sacred and untainted virtues. But when its Divine passion is stilled and its ardent yearning slackens, it retraces its course from the realm of the Divine and becomes man,

THE MYSTICISM OF PHILO

lighting upon those human interests which lie in wait for it at the entrance of the sanctuary" (*De Somn.* ii. 232 ff.). This means that the spirit is too frail to keep itself so firmly concentrated on God and so completely alienated from material concerns as to be able to retain its full Divine illumination.

Hence we are not surprised to find repeated hints in Philo that the grasp of the Existent in ecstasy is a rare attainment. No doubt he has frequent descriptions of the τέλειος, the man who has reached the goal and may be called "completely a man of God." But when we look deeper we can discern that he reserves this high designation for a favoured few. It holds good without reservation of Abraham and Moses. But in the main it stands for an ideal which towers high above the aspirations of humanity.

At this point, as at so many, the position of Philo is strikingly elucidated by the mystical experience of Plotinus. Apparently by this famous mystic the estatic state was rarely enjoyed. Dean Inge, in drawing a most illuminating contrast between Plotinus

THE MYSTICISM OF PHILO

and later mystics such as Böhme and Blake, points out that while Böhme, for example, used to hypnotise himself to induce abnormal spiritual conditions, Plotinus always insisted that the Divine vision must be waited for (*Philosophy of Plotinus*, ii. 152 f.). This meant a patient quieting of the soul, of which but few are capable.

Philo's outlook is, in essentials, the same. We might almost venture to say that the catena of extracts so skilfully linked together by Dr. Inge (*op. cit.* ii. pp. 132–142) to illustrate the fundamental character of the mysticism of Plotinus, except for modifications here and there in the interest of Jewish monotheism, unfolds to us the very essence of Philo's mystic ecstasy.

That ecstasy is the crowning-point of a religious experience which may well create in the unprejudiced student of Philo a willing and affectionate reverence. He will carry away from his acquaintance with the Alexandrian sage a feeling like that which Dr. Rendel Harris so sympathetically describes when speaking of his own work on

THE MYSTICISM OF PHILO

the Fragments. "To us," he says (*Fragments of Philo*, p. 1 f.), "his fragments are no mere chaff and draff, but such blessed brokenness of truth just dawning on the world that one would imagine him to be holding out to us what had previously passed through the hands of the Master Himself." To these words the present writer can whole-heartedly say, Amen.

INDEX

(1) AUTHORS AND SUBJECTS

Abraham, 33, 34, 41, 46, 122, 123, 124, 133, 138, 199, 231, 235.
Advocate (παράκλητος), 113, 114.
Alexandria, 8, 19, 38, 159, 176, 177.
Allegory, 2, 25, 32, 33, 34, 35, 36, 38, 40, 48.
Angels, 6, 80, 159, 162.
Archer Hind, 73.
Arnim, Von, 24.
Aucher, 24, 164, 182, 224.

Barker, E., 63.
Bigg, 123, 185, 215.
Blake, W., 236.
Body, 75, 86, 88, 98, 99.
Böhme, 236.
Bousset, 8, 38, 78, 213, 219, 222.
Bréhier, 53, 54, 58, 77, 108, 112, 125, 140, 165, 218, 219.

Cicero, 53.
Clement of Alexandria, 36.
Cohn, 24, 25, 138, 153.
Compendia, 2, 9.
Conscience, 27, 53, 106 ff., 111, 114, 115, 116 f., 146.
Creation, 64, 65, 76.

Diaspora, 19, 21, 151.

Diogenes Laertius, 64, 188.
Drummond, J., 53, 69, 71, 170, 180, 189.
Dualism, 70, 73.

Ecstasy, 199, 205, 210, 214, 217 f., 221, 223 ff., 229, 230, 231, 233.
Education (Greek), 7, 10, 13, 19.
Egyptian theology, 219.
Ephesus, 177.
Epicharmus, 105.
Epistles (Pauline), 20.
Ezekiel, 160.
ἔλεγχος, 107, 108, 114.

Faith, 27, 122, 125, 126, 127, 131–134, 215 f., 217.
Fathers (Christian), 1, 58.
Flesh (σάρξ), 74, 89, 90, 94.
Fourth Gospel, 20, 37, 47–50, 176.

Geffcken, 2.
God, relation of, to world, 62 f.; as Creator, 64 f., 67, 84 f.; and necessity, 73; man's longing for, 96 ff., 193; relation of, to Lord, 144; generosity of, 154, 155; transcendence of, 160; Spirit of, 27, 172, 184, 187, 190;

INDEX

as Father, 179 ff., 184; immediate apprehension of, 207, 209, 235.
Grace (Divine), 17, 27, 59, 117, 142, 143, 145, 147, 148 f., 152, 153, 156.

Harris, Rendel, 176, 236.
Hatch, E., 58.
Hatch, W. H. P., 125.
Hebrews (Epistle to), 20, 124, 134, 162, 170.
Heinze, 69.
Hellenism, 7, 8, 13, 19, 21, 26, 31, 76, 140, 214, 218, 219, 226.
Heraclitus, 177.
Hermetic documents, 61, 158, 219.
Hope, 119.

Ideas (Platonic), 64, 67, 158.
Immortality, 9, 134, 137, 138, 140, 141.
Inge, W. R., 225, 235, 236.
Inspiration (verbal), 32, 37, 38, 39, 40, 44; prophetic, 226, 227, 233.

Jeremiah, 56, 112.
Jesus, 6, 22, 154, 181, 182.
Jowett, 23.

Kroll, J., 61, 184.

Law, (Mosaic), 2, 30, 31, 44, 45, 51, 54, 56.
Leckie, J. H., 141.
Lietzmann, H., 89.
Life, 135, 137.
Lightfoot, 41.
Logos, 5, 6, 27, 79, 84, 85, 87, 109, 161, 162, 163, 167–169, 170, 172 f., 176 f., 186, 189, 192.
λόγοι, 67, 158, 166, 169.

Man, Ideal, in Philo, 76, 78; in Paul, 78, 79.
Mangey, 133.
Markland, 66, 204.
Matter, 62, 64, 65, 66, 67, 68, 70, 71, 72, 74.
Mechilta, 122.
Mediators, 27, 157 ff.
Mêmrâ, 160.
Moses, 2, 3, 29, 30, 51, 57, 63, 64, 155, 200, 212, 220, 231, 235.
Mystery-terminology, 34, 212, 213, 220.
Mysticism, 211 ff., 214.
Myth, 39.

Neo-Pythagoreanism, 60, 89.
New Testament, 20, 184, 191.

Old Testament, in Christian theology, 4; in Philo, 18 f., 25, 46, 62, 83, 122, 180, 188.
οὐσία, relation of, to ὕλη, 67, 69.

Panaetius, 53.
Passions, 100, 101.
Paul, 26, 40, 41, 42, 43, 56, 58, 131 f., 134, 135, 136, 138, 141, 149, 150 f., 183, 191, 206 f., 215.
Peter, 7.
Phaedrus, 188.
Philo, use of, by Fathers, 1, 2; date of, 6; traditions regarding, 7; and Hellenism, 7; style of, 10; personality of, 10–15; culture of, 12, 13, 14; poetic strain in, 15 ff.; religion of, 1, 6, 22, 23; verbal minutiae in, 37; and Posidonius, 61; syncretism of, 61, 79; his experiences of spiritual illumination, 203 ff.; opposition of, to mystic initiation, 220.

INDEX

Philosophy of Philo, 1, 5, 19, 22, 25, 60.
Plato, 2, 18, 60, 62, 64, 65, 70, 72, 73, 74, 80, 158, 180.
Pleasure, 100.
Plotinus, 215, 219, 225, 235, 236.
Plutarch, 219.
Posidonius, 53, 61.
Powers (Divine), 5, 6, 162, 164, 165, 166, 169, 208.
Prayer, 225, 226.
Pre-existence (of Souls), 80.
Prophets, 57, 58, 226, 227, 228.
παρρησία, 129, 130 f.
πνευματικός, 92.
ψυχικός, 92, 93.

Reason (νοῦς), 81, 83, 84, 85, 87, 91, 93, 94, 106 f., 147, 186.
Redemption, 89, 148.
Reitzenstein, 213, 218, 219.
Repentance, 27, 116 ff., 121.
Revelation, 1, 193.
Ritual, 54, 55.
Ryle, 39, 57.

Schlatter, 126.
Schmekel, 9, 53, 60.
Schürer, 50.
Self-love, 102.
Seneca, 64.
Septuagint, 31, 32, 38.
Shekinah, 160.
Siegfried, 32, 62, 70, 71, 161.
Sin, 27, 72, 81, 98, 101, 104.
Sonship, 179, 180 f.
Soul (ψυχή), 75, 86, 87, 90, 91, 92.

Spinoza, 216.
Spirit (πνεῦμα), 75, 84, 87, 90, 91, 92, 94, 95, 185.
Stoics, 2, 5, 9, 52, 60, 63, 67, 74, 86, 112, 125, 158, 183, 188.
Supplication, 152, 153, 169, 170.
Symbolism, 48, 49.
Synagogue, 59.
Syncretism, 60, 79.

Thompson, J. M., 48.
Thoth, 158.
Timaeus, 61, 63, 65, 69, 70, 73, 80, 86.
τέλειος, 120, 235.
τροπή, 105.

Underhill, E., 217.
Union (with God), 27, 28, 178 ff.
Ur-Anthropos, 78.
ὑποδοχή, 69, 70.
ὑπόληψις, 126.

Vanity (τῦφος), 103, 105.
Vision of God, 192 ff.; conditions of, 194 ff.; Philo's conception of, 198–202.

Webb, C. C. J., 216.
Wendland, P., 24, 208.
Windisch, H., 57, 101, 178.
Wisdom, 9, 62, 159, 162, 173, 174.
Wisdom of Solomon, 8, 159.

Zeller, 70, 80, 189, 210.

INDEX

(2) REFERENCES IN PHILO

(Paragraphs numbered as in Cohn and Wendland's ed.)

De Opificio Mundi—	PAGE
3	52
8 f.	63
16	65
21	66
23	72
24 f.	163
45–52, 89–106	48
66	93
73	101
77	178
134	76
139	84
146	109
169	104, 148

Legum Allegoriarum Libri i.—	
5	66
22	66
34	147
37 f.	84, 185
48 f.	149
65	173
82 ff.	222
97	93
107	136

Leg. Alleg. ii.—	
19	39
22	93
31	223
85	93

Leg. Alleg. iii.—	
3	219
27	97
41 f.	194
47	193
64	100
68	100
71	98
73	86
78	146
96	163

Leg. Alleg. iii.—contd.	PAGE
100	201, 213
105 f.	148
129	101
139	219
145	93
161	75
171	93
207	172
209	34
211	99, 100, 117
215	154

De Cherubim—	
27 ff.	34, 144
37 f.	12
42 ff.	55, 219
48	212
49	179
81 ff.	13
130	13

De Sacrificiis Abelis et Caini—	
5	138
8	175
60	212
123	13

Quod Deterius Potiori insidiari soleat—	
13	36
22 f.	107
70	93
72 f.	14
82–90	81
83	186
84	94
95	152
97	101
109	88
122	101
139	76
148 f.	104
158 f.	195

INDEX

De Posteritate Caini—

	PAGE
15	200
22	12
27	197
31	97
59	114
105 f.	13
142	155
145	155
169	166

De Gigantibus—

6-15	80
20 ff.	188
23	95
29	90
40	90
47	190
52	225
53	190
54	213
54 f.	191
61	140
210 f.	113

Quod Deus sit immutabilis—

38 f.	12
65	13
72	100
76	145
82 f.	175
87	226
123	137
134 ff.	109

De Agricultura—

1 ff.	37
9	107
49 f.	154
96 f.	39
111 ff.	13
136	14

De Plantatione—

18	164, 186
22 ff.	198
32 ff.	32
37	139
89	145

De Ebrietate—

	PAGE
44	12
49 ff.	13
89	13
147	223

De Sobrietate—

56	183

De Confusione Linguarum—

41	170
97	96
134 f.	35
135 f.	35
145	181
146	170, 182

De Migratione Abrahami—

2	205
6	12
9	89
30 ff.	149, 224
32	49
34 f.	204
43 f.	133
57	169
89	36, 55
90	56
96	56
102	162
136 f.	106
169	179
170 f.	199
173 ff.	169
181	165
193	179

Quis Rerum Divinarum Heres sit—

19	130
21	123
26 ff.	130
29	115
31	17, 155
55 ff.	186
69 f.	17, 205, 222
73	86
79	173
90 ff.	129

INDEX

Quis Rerum Divinarum Heres sit—continued

	PAGE
93	126
101	125
106 ff.	102
160	67, 68
205	167
255	95
265	190
268	88
273	153
276	138

De Congressu Eruditionis Gratia—

11–24	41
15 ff.	13
67 f.	14

De Fuga et Inventione—

12 f.	163
28 ff.	14
54 f.	37
55	137
58	138
66 ff.	165
69 f.	85
90 ff.	232
101	161
108 ff.	162
131	107
141	194
177 f.	49
182	94
203 f.	113

De Mutatione Nominum—

9 f.	201
49	100
58 f.	146
65	49
82	192
129	145
138	150
161 f.	18

De Somniis i.—

9	153
62	164
66	166

De Somniis i.—*continued*

	PAGE
73	33
76	68
86	172
91	115
92 f.	43
103 ff.	171
142	166
143	166
148	197
151 f.	139
163	144
181	148
232	196
236	196

De Somniis ii.—

45	79
48 ff.	14
61–68	48
232 ff.	235
242 ff.	173
252	189
353	73

De Abrahamo—

8	119
26	120
41	102
47	120
55	135
58	192
79 f.	200
99	33
119 ff.	208
151	14
156 ff.	12
167–199	36
200	34
263	128
268 f.	122, 128

De Josepho—

1–27	36
15	49
32 ff.	14
47 f.	112
54 ff.	14
189	49
265	182

INDEX

De Vita Mosis i.—	PAGE
4	50
84, 222-226	50

De Vita Mosis ii. (iii.)—	
6	228
14	51
36	31
40	31
48	53
103	33
147	72, 100
187 f.	30
238	147
239	17

De Decalogo—	
5 ff.	103
18-31	48
87	108
134	75

De Specialibus Legibus i.—	
36	96
43	156
207	198
235 ff.	113, 116
260 (= *De Sacrific.*)	42
266	86
271	54
281 f.	151
307	144
318	182
319	220
328 f.	67

De Spec. Leg. iii.—	
1 ff.	12
4-6	16
161	88

De Spec. Leg. iv.—	
49 f.	227
75	93
123	87
192	226

De Virtutibus—	PAGE
145 f.	43
169	157
175 ff.	121
177	120
188	147
216	123

De Praemiis et Poenis—	
15	119
26	199
27, 30, 49	134
37 ff.	202
39	184
70	136
116	153

De Exsecrationibus—	
163	118

Legatio ad Gaium—	
5	193
6 f.	164

Quaestiones in Genesim i.—	
82	118
92	182

Quaestiones in Genesim ii.—	
42 f.	121

Quaestiones in Genesim iii.—	
9	231
190 f.	41

Quaestiones in Genesim iv.—	
1	203
4	234
64	101
140	224
203	105

Quaestiones in Exodum i.—	
15	117

Quaestiones in Exodum ii.—	
29	233
51	206
68	164

www.ingramcontent.com/pod-product-compliance
Lightning Source LLC
Chambersburg PA
CBHW071428150426
43191CB00008B/1077